# Pitch Yourself

# Books to make you better

Books to make you better. To make you *be* better, *do* better, *feel* better. Whether you want to upgrade your personal skills or change your job, whether you want to improve your managerial style, become a more powerful communicator, or be stimulated and inspired as you work.

*Prentice Hall Business* is leading the field with a new breed of skills, careers and development books. Books that are a cut above the mainstream – in topic, content and delivery – with an edge and verve that will make you better, with less effort.

Books that are as sharp and smart as you are.

*Prentice Hall Business.*
We work harder – so you don't have to.

For more details on products, and to contact us, visit
**www.business-minds.com**
**www.yourmomentum.com**

# Pitch
# Yourself

## Stand out from the CV crowd with a Personal Elevator Pitch

Bill Faust and Michael Faust

*an imprint of* Pearson Education

London • New York • Toronto • Sydney • Tokyo • Singapore • Hong Kong • Cape Town

New Delhi • Madrid • Paris • Amsterdam • Munich • Milan • Stockholm

650.14
FAU

PEARSON EDUCATION LIMITED

Head Office:
Edinburgh Gate
Harlow CM20 2JE
Tel: +44 (0)1279 623623
Fax: +44 (0)1279 431059

London Office:
128 Long Acre
London WC2E 9AN
Tel: +44 (0)20 7447 2000
Fax: +44 (0)20 7447 2170
Website: www.business-minds.com

First published in Great Britain in 2002

ISBN 0 273 66171 X

British Library Cataloguing in Publication Data
A CIP catalogue record for this book can be obtained from the British Library

10 9 8 7 6 5 4 3 2 1

Designed by Claire Brodmann Book Designs, Lichfield, Staffs.
Typeset by Northern Phototypesetting Co. Ltd, Bolton
Printed and bound in Great Britain by Bell & Bain Ltd, Glasgow

The Publishers' policy is to use paper manufactured from sustainable forests.

To Sophie my girlfriend and Brighton Beach.
*Bill*

Thanks to my wife Kimi and to the lost autumn days and nights.
*Michael*

# Acknowledgements

The kernel of this book was generated by the positive reaction from those people who were unexpectedly exposed to the early versions of the Elevator Pitch. Thank you.

We would also like to thank friends and colleagues who acted as sounding boards and were kind enough to let us use their life experiences. They acted as both judge and jury. Without them our words would be poorer.

John Baldwin, Ken Livingstone, Justine Cobb, Mara Goldstein, Nancy Prendergast, Richard Davies, Jack Gratton, Mark Bailey, Charlie Dobres, Kate Marsh, Marc Schavemaker, Darren Fell, Louise Medley, Laura Neilson.

# Contents

# The rallying cry

"The CV is dead. Long live the CV!

There has to be a better way. The purpose of a CV in my opinion is simply to get you in front of a prospective employer. It should therefore be short and sharp without introducing negatives. That's where the problems start to arise. You are judged on a piece of paper, which can't portray the real you. Using the Elevator Pitch technique is a brilliant way to put over your case quickly and succinctly.

I hope it becomes the industry standard."

Jack Gratton, Founder and CEO of Major Players, the UK's leading marketing and services recruitment agency

# Introduction

Over the last 100 years, the CV has become a standard world currency that is now debased by the changes in our work patterns and environments. The CV is dead. The Elevator Pitch takes off where the CV stops. The Elevator Pitch is the 21st century successor to the CV.

In today's world, you need to constantly market yourself at each and every point in your career path. You might be a graduate or have 15 years' line-management experience, or perhaps you are returning to work after a family career break, or even making a functional change or jumping to a new industry sector. Each break and renewed step requires you to sell yourself. Over and over again.

Ask yourself the following questions. Is my CV the hard-hitting sales tool I think and hope it is? Does a functional, linear and ultimately historical view of my career sell the real me? Can I see the real me in the words of my CV? Does my CV really explain what I can deliver in the future and showcase my abilities?

Unfortunately, the answer is invariably no. The CV is a straitjacket on your next career move rather than a life jacket. The CV is like a rococo building: it's so rich and opulent that you miss the reason it was built. As a sales tool it tries to communicate everything. It focuses on the wrong issues as it begins from the seller's reality rather than the buyer's perspective. It is what you have done and where you have done it. You often forget that a CV is meant to get you through the door, not do the interview as well. The

CV shrouds your career in the past. It hides your core worth, your ability to deliver in the future within a new work environment, beneath the historical and functional façade of your career. Consequently the CV needs to be deciphered to get underneath this façade yet we do not provide the key. We allow people to make snap judgements about us based on this outmoded document. The CV has stood in a time warp for over 100 years while the world has moved on.

Why write a CV if the CV is dead? Perhaps it's down to those 100 years of convention and tradition. But then you don't give a fig about being hidebound to tradition, do you? Maybe it's time to step back and think about a better way to show what you've really got to offer.

The Elevator Pitch is the better way. The Elevator Pitch is the 21st century replacement of the CV. The Elevator Pitch is not about incremental improvements to a CV. There are many books we'd gladly recommend for that.

Rather, the Elevator Pitch is a fundamental and lateral rethink of what is required to sell you in today's market. The Elevator Pitch debunks the CV of its extraneous wrappings and conventional padding by jettisoning the historical and functional veneer of your career. Instead the Elevator Pitch focuses on your unique set of behaviours, abilities and skills, sometimes referred to as competencies, that help define how you will perform in a new job under a new set of circumstances. The Elevator Pitch demonstrates your value and worth by showing who you are and how you have done it

The Elevator Pitch focuses on the things your buyer is looking for. It successfully differentiates you through selective communication. You control the agenda and the speed at which key information is released through the negotiating phase. The Elevator Pitch allows you to cut to the chase. Time is not wasted. The Elevator Pitch provides a common language of understanding. Effective recruitment decisions will be faster and easier.

The Elevator Pitch is the only sales tool you need, after yourself.

It is focused, highly targeted, concise and proven to work. It is usually just one page.

The aim of this book is to introduce the Elevator Pitch. You will be provided with the essential tools to create your own personal Elevator Pitch. We will show you how to discover and understand your Transferable Assets: those behaviours, skills and abilities that define and predict your performance. We then show you how to construct and write your own personal Elevator Pitch and how to position yourself in an overcrowded and overcommunicated society.

Welcome to the non-stop, ever-changing world. Welcome to reality. Welcome to the Elevator Pitch.

chapter 1

# The death of the CV

# Think and act differently

'When the world zigs, zag' is the mantra of the world's best known and most fêted advertising agencys, BBH, based in London. Their philosophy is to look at the world from a new vantage point by thinking and acting differently.

They are not alone. The Onassis oil dynasty, Apple, Warren Buffet, Virgin, South West Airlines in the USA and easyJet in the UK have all zagged while the world zigged. Indeed, we also probably all know a friend or a colleague whom we secretly admire for their ability to zag when we still zig.

These people, and others like them, have stepped off from the world, taken a back seat, viewed it from afar, jumbled it into a new perspective, and then got on ahead of us. Their view of the world helps frame and change ours. They challenge common assumptions. They throw normal convention out of the window. They are willing to step outside their comfort zone. They are willing to be counted. They are not afraid to push boundaries and question conventional or traditional wisdom. They have done things differently. They are doing things differently. They aim to stand out, create value and be successful.

They want to challenge not just for the sake of the challenge but because there is a better way.

So the question you must ask yourself is simple: do you want to stand afresh and zag, or do you want to be boring and zig?

# Do you zig or zag?

To find out how willing and able you are to zag when others zig, answer the following questions:

→ Do you believe that in our overcommunicated and hectic society, the key to being noticed is to communicate selectively and not try to communicate everything?

→ Do you believe that you buy goods and services, including hiring people, on both rational (objective) and emotional (subjective) grounds?

→ Do you believe that time is only one of the factors that create emotional and spiritual growth?

→ Do you want to realize your individual potential rather than simply fill a job market vacancy?

→ Are you an individual, not simply a number, within a company hierarchy?

→ Do you want to find the job to fit you?

→ Do you wish to enjoy your career?

→ Are you loyal and true to yourself rather than waiting for the company to be loyal to you?

→ Do you believe that changes in organizations impact on the type of career you will have?

→ Do you believe that people searching for vertical ladders in a horizontal career game will, more often than not, lose?

→ Do you have a defined view of how your career will start, progress and continue?

→ Are you happy with variety?

→ Are you likely to want several careers, not just one? Do you have a choice?

→ Do you want to find a job where the demands of the job fit you, not one where your job-related knowledge simply matches the job description?

➡ Are you brave enough to sell your future worth rather than relying on previous achievements?

➡ Do you want the market to buy you?

If you found yourself saying 'yes' you're ready to begin

## Your sales tool

What are you using to sell yourself? No doubt it's your CV. What does your CV say about you? If you are not there, what impression does the reader get? Does it sell you? Would you buy you?

Worryingly we know that despite all your efforts, your CV will look similar to many others. Few actually stand out. The CV is a straitjacket. It is normally in reverse chronological order. It is based on function. It's autobiographical. The CV provides a linear, one-dimensional perspective to you. It is fact and form. It is rational and safe. It is what you are and what you have been. It is historical. It is an inventory of your jobs. It is simply a catalogue.

Let's look at the basic CV structure. Many CVs are similar to those in Figure 1.1, which shows a simple success story: a career within one function, such as accountancy or marketing, over a couple of industries,

# Would you
# buy you?

| Job | Function | Industry sector | |
|---|---|---|---|
| Board director | Function x | Industry B | |
| Director | Function x | Industry A | |
| Manager | Function x | Industry A | |
| Graduate | Function x | Industry A | |

Reverse chronology

Most ← Least
Hierarchy of emphasis

**Figure 1.1**   The CV stripped bare

with a steady progression through the job ranks presented in reverse chronological order. The CV presents and uses criteria such as length of employment, job title, qualifications, number of people managed, and budgets managed as prima facie evidence of your capability.

Several of you will have gone a step further. Let's look at the same basic CV where you have quantified some results. You might also add a career mission statement. You throw down some good-sounding adjectives from a thesaurus. You make it rational and logical. You forget that the world turns on emotions. You take up lots of room describing job roles. You may even have created several objective–analysis– action–result scenarios; you construct a basic SWOT (strengths, weaknesses, opportunities, threats) analysis on yourself; you pry into your 360-degree assessments; you look long and hard at your Belbin or Myers Briggs profiles. And after this soul searching, you include a list of how you made things happen around yourself. This is shown in Figure 1.2 – a familiar sight to many of you.

So you have fine-tuned your CV. You are happy. You have a catalogue of your career history. Yet too many CVs are wrong. They are wrong for many reasons.

| Job | Function | Industry sector | Results | |
|-----|----------|-----------------|---------|---|
| Board director | Function *x* | Industry B | Results A<br>Results B | Reverse chronology |
| Director | Function *x* | Industry A | Results A<br>Results B | |
| Manager | Function *x* | Industry A | Results A<br>Results B | |
| Graduate | Function *x* | Industry A | Results A<br>Results B | |

Most ⟵ —————————————————— Least

Hierarchy of emphasis

**Figure 1.2**   The better CV stripped bare

## First, basic mistakes are made

A recent survey by FirstPersonGlobal, the UK's leading online executive recruitment service dedicated to technology professionals, and part of Harvey Nash, looked at 200 CVs submitted in response to two separate Harvey Nash recruitment campaigns, one searching for an IT director for a financial services company and the other searching for a marketing director for an Internet company. Each CV was reviewed against four criteria: readability, impression, page length and relevance.

Amazingly, 31% of these CVs made so many basic mistakes that they were considered poor and only 19% of all the CVs submitted made no

# competencies
# your future

mistakes. Just over four out of every ten CVs had issues with structure and therefore understanding, and nearly one-quarter were over three pages long, putting undue pressure on the reader. Crucially 34% of the CVs could not answer the question, 'what does this person actually do and where have they done it?' And 23% showed evidence of incorrectly prioritizing less relevant information.

So one in three CVs could not answer what this person does, and over one in five could not prioritize correctly. You could say that this is a pretty sad state of affairs. This research is not an isolated example. You probably know of some more. You have probably seen it on CVs you have seen when recruiting. You can therefore conclude that many CVs, and potentially yours, do not even do the basic job expected of them.

### Second, and worse, the CV actually hides what you are selling

Behind the results you have just added to your CV lie the traits and behaviours that enabled you to deliver these results successfully in the first place. These are your competencies. Results don't evidence the role you were in, but they do evidence your competencies within a given context. In other words, competencies really define your future worth and capability, as they are your fundamental building blocks. Competencies aid understanding of the behaviour patterns that make

## really define
## worth and
## capability

an individual successful in a given environment. Understanding your own competencies allows you to answer the questions, 'Who am I?' and 'Why am I who I am?' Competencies have existed ever since man first walked the earth. Why is one person a better hunter than another? What made this person the leader during a crisis and their adversary a leader during a period of consolidation? What made Shackleton inspirational to his lost men? What drives entrepreneurs? Why do some people take risk? What makes a great teacher? Why do mountaineers continually push themselves?

The CV is not good at showcasing competencies. Your CV hides your fundamental building blocks behind a criteria-based chronological façade. This is shown in Figure 1.3.

So, a criteria-based CV shows what you have done and where you have done it, rather than who you are and how you have done it. Look at Figure 1.4, which illustrates the flawed CV.

| Job | Function | Industry sector | Results | Competencies |
|---|---|---|---|---|
| Board director | Function *x* | Industry B | Results A<br>Results B | Competency 1<br>Competency 2<br>3<br>4<br>5<br>6 |
| Director | Function *x* | Industry A | Results C<br>Results D | |
| Manager | Function *x* | Industry A | Results E<br>Results F | |
| Graduate | Function *x* | Industry A | Results G<br>Results H | |

What you expose to the world
(What you write on your CV)

What you hide from the world
(What you do not write on your CV)

**Figure 1.3**   The errant CV

## Third, CVs aren't customer friendly

Let's place ourselves in our customer's shoes. What are you selling? What are they buying? How do you bridge the gap to establish common ground?

Funky Business, a treatise on our new world order of funk has this rallying cry

**"The moral: what companies sell and what their customers buy are two different things. Therefore, every once in a while it is wise to place yourself in the shoes of your customers and ask the question: 'What are they really buying?' The answer, 99 times out of 100, is not what you think you are selling."**

Recruitment agencies are one of your many customer bases. Whether you like it or not, recruitment companies work for the employer and not the employee. Indeed, there is a fundamental conflict between the recruitment industry's imperative to fill vacancies and the need by candidates to take control of their careers. Recruitment agencies fit people into jobs not find jobs for people.

The aim of the recruitment process is to minimize the risk of hiring rather than maximize the opportunity for the employer and successful applicant. Risk is minimized by using two broad filters, criteria

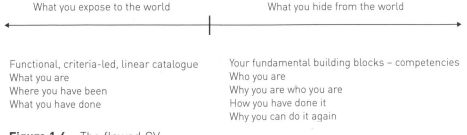

What you expose to the world      What you hide from the world

Functional, criteria-led, linear catalogue     Your fundamental building blocks – competencies
What you are     Who you are
Where you have been     Why you are who you are
What you have done     How you have done it
     Why you can do it again

**Figure 1.4**   The flawed CV

# recruitment for the employer

(schooling, qualifications, time in job, number of people managed ...) and competencies.

Think about this for a short while and your own experience of the recruitment process. Which is more important and which is easier to acquire? Surely it would make sense to hire for core motivation and traits first and foremost, as these are more difficult to acquire than skills and knowledge? Absolutely.

So why do so many companies appear to do the reverse, and why do so many recruitment companies not advise them any better? It might be down to the way recruitment takes place. Many of us have probably been through a relatively unstructured recruitment process, where discussions have meandered and you have never got past talking superficially about yourself. In this instance, you have probably gone no deeper than the criteria signposted on your CV.

On other occasions, you will have read an ad, met the recruitment consultant, seen the brief, and undergone a structured interview. The goal of a competency-based structured interview is to estimate what people will do under a given set of circumstances and to determine what skills and attributes they will bring to the position. This is achieved by encouraging the interviewee, you, to share examples of your past behaviour and describe how this experience can be applied to future situations. This also

# companies work and not the employee

places an onus on the interviewer to be prepared and understand what competencies they are seeking and so increase the chance of a great hiring. Competencies form a common language that helps reinforce a company's culture and helps you establish whether you like the company.

During the interview you share a number of experiences until you unlock the hidden depths of your career as though you were peeling the layers from an onion. You go past the criteria based functional and historical veneer of your CV to showcase your base motives, traits and competencies. You can only do this because the interviewer, through their questioning, probes aspects of your behaviour and so provides the key to decipher your CV and therefore gain an understanding of what makes you tick. They are wanting to know the value you will add to their company in the future.

Your CV needs to be deciphered to showcase your career and your future value. Your CV can only be deciphered through a structured competency based interview. What happens when you are confronted by an unstructured interview? Why do you lock your career into the straitjacket of a CV? Why are you hiding your competencies behind the traditional CV façade and veneer? Why are you missing out on a huge opportunity to gain an advantage? What happens when you are not there to guide the recruitment agency, say at the shortlisting stage?

The initial gatekeeping decision to shortlist you appears to be based around your criteria and not your competencies. This might have something to do with time and tradition. Criteria have existed for hundreds of years and have been codified by the CV in the last 100 years. Similarly, competencies have been around for hundreds of years yet only codified since the mid 1990s. You might say that you use a CV because everyone else does. Just because it has been done this way for so long does not mean it must be good. Just because something is familiar, tried and tested, and therefore understood within a certain context and accepted by certain people, does not necessarily mean it fulfils the many diverse needs or demands placed upon it. Tradition is not always correct. There is a constant flow of new ideas. Our written and spoken language does not stay static. It changes. The Swiss army knife has given way to the Leatherman. The Hoover has given way to the Dyson. The Filofax has been replaced by the Palm Pilot. The desk diary has been replaced by Microsoft Outlook.

The reality is that competencies are often used in hiring. Using competencies ensures that better hiring decisions are made. The competencies that are analyzed are defined by the organization's competency matrix. The problem is that CVs don't highlight competencies, so shortlisting, the critical start to any job, remains the most inaccurate part of the recruitment process. But you can improve the shortlisting process.

# because it has this way for mean it must

Jim Bright and Joanne Earl are two prominent organizational psychologists, based in Australia, who consult and write extensively on career development, selection, testing and training. Their recent book is a culmination of years of dedicated research into what makes a winning candidate and CV based on interviews with hundreds of recruiters across a wide industry spectrum. One of the areas they looked at was the inclusion and exclusion of competency statements, and how this impacted on the decision by these recruiters to shortlist and interview a candidate. The results were startling and also consistent:

**"[We] were amazed to find that, when we included them [competency statements] ... they boosted our candidates' chances by as much as 30 per cent ... The more competency statements you put on ... the more chance you have of being short listed ..."**

Conclusive and concrete evidence that competency statements provided at an early stage in the recruitment process, i.e. before shortlisting even begins, make a real difference. The difference between a yes vote and a no vote. The difference in shortlisting. The difference between an interview and no interview. The difference between landing a new job and returning to your existing one. The difference in being noticed.

We've established that CVs lack focus. They concentrate on criteria rather than competencies. However, the interview process focuses on

been done
so long does not
be good

both criteria and competencies. At some stage, there is a change in emphasis from criteria to competencies. But you are currently letting other people work this transition out for you. Figure 1.5 illustrates this contradiction. The wider the shaded area, the greater the emphasis.

We can illustrate this point further and the difference between criteria and competencies by considering the lonely hearts pages found in newspapers and magazines (Figure 1.6).

Both the CV and the lonely hearts ads are trying to be alluring and sell the benefits of you to another person. Both are laid out in a familiar and unique format, both carry stock phrases and both are a suggested length.

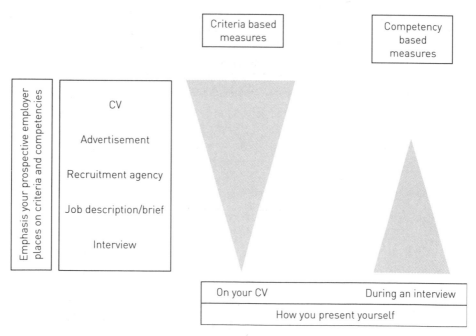

**Figure 1.5**   The CV's emphasis is flawed

**Figure 1.6** The CV is a lonely heart

Think of some lonely hearts ads. If you've never looked at one, grab a newspaper and analyze them carefully. Our guess is that over 80% of them describe only the physical characteristics of the person sought. They might say, 'Tall, dark and handsome educated man sought by, Latin, well-travelled female who is into walks in the country and cinema.' It doesn't exactly help you understand her emotional make-up, the character of the person she would like to meet, or why they might actually have a bright future. Think back to your CV. The well-travelled, Latin female is equivalent to the top part of a CV, where many people include a number of adjectives describing themselves, such as, 'professional salesperson with ten years' experience managing clients across international borders'. The tall, dark, handsome section is the equivalent of your own criteria-based historical catalogue of your career (Figure 1.7). Where do you attempt to explain what makes you tick and why you would be a good fit for a company?

CVs are also unfocused in their overall message. CVs need to be more relevant, pertinent and accessible.

| | CV | Lonely hearts |
|---|---|---|
| Format | Ad to sell yourself | Ad to sell yourself |
| Length | 2–3 pages | 10–16 lines |
| Focus on what you want | Career mission statement | Criteria (wanted: tall, dark, handsome …) |
| Focus on what you are | Adjectives describing yourself (professional) salesperson with ten years' experience managing clients …) Criteria-based career catalogue (company X for five years, rising to junior sales assistant …) | Criteria (sought by: curvy, petite female …) |

**Figure 1.7**   CV versus lonely hearts

The CV is a blunderbuss (Figure 1.8). The CV throws mud at a wall, hoping some will stick. However, mud flinging is a fine art. Just because more mud is thrown at a given wall does not mean that a greater proportion sticks (Figure 1.9). The CV is too generic to communicate well.

Think back to FirstPersonGlobal's research. They want you to provide the answer to their questions, 'What does this person do or offer me? Where is their value add?' They want this answered, rightly or wrongly, in a fast and furious (and generous) 90 seconds, without you being there. Think about what this means for you. The onus is on you to communicate not then to understand. In order to communicate you need to provide pertinent, relevant and accessible information. In other words you need to be selective in how you describe yourself.

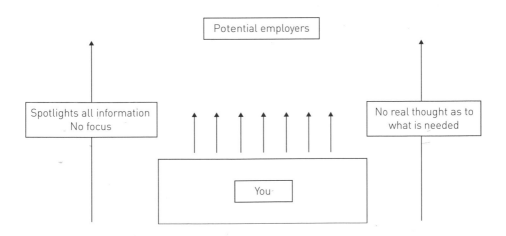

**Figure 1.8**   You – the blunderbuss

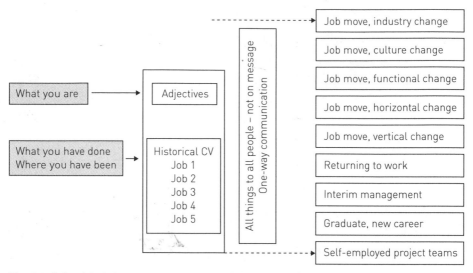

**Figure 1.9**  Mud thrown – some will stick

Every product sold has an angle or positioning in the marketplace. This is the most motivating and differentiating thing a manufacturer can say about the product. By its very nature, it cannot be all things to all people. The angle can be unearthed from one of many sources.

➡ Product characteristics, e.g. ingredients, texture, availability, country of origin.

➡ User characteristics, e.g. experts use it, celebrities use it, competent DIY-ers use it.

➡ Ways of using the product, e.g. sharing, indulgence, giving.

➡ Price characteristics, e.g. value, price, cheap, expensive.

➡ Image characteristics, e.g. being friendly, offering quality, being serious.

➡ Product heritage, e.g. established in, matured since.

➡ Direct comparison, e.g. the Coke/Pepsi challenge.

➡ Newsworthiness shown by topical anniversaries.

➡ And many more category areas.

You'll notice that some of the sources of positioning can be rational, whereas others are much more emotional, richer and more resonant. Try and think about some of your favourite brands and what they stand for. It's relatively easy for the big global brands but what about the tea you are drinking, the biscuits you are eating, the batteries in your torch, the pen you are writing with, the computer you are using, the watch you are wearing, the chocolates you shared at a dinner party, your kitchen cleaner, your toothpaste, your favourite fizzy drink, the mobile phone shop, your favourite website to the jacket you are wearing?

You can probably think of a catchphrase or strapline for many of these brands or at least a collection of sentences that sum up what they are. But, most importantly, whatever the words, they will have a meaning that is relevant, accessible and personal to you.

So positioning satisfies a consumer need as it addresses why a brand is relevant for that consumer. At the heart of positioning is selective communication. Positioning is customer-centric not supplier-centric. Positioning is the bottom rung on a Maslowian hierarchy of communication needs. Correct positioning identifies the core dimensions of relevance and prioritization leading to understanding and comprehension.

How often have you written your CV from your perspective rather than from your customer's perspective? When did you last ask yourself what constitutes relevant information? What does my potential employer want to know about me? We've seen that criteria are important but not that important. Should criteria or competencies form your positioning or angle? Why did you write a CV if you had no angle?

We have seen that CVs are flawed. The first flaw arises because they do not focus on the buyer or answer their needs for relevant, succinct and pertinent information. A catalogue is not a dialogue and lacks engagement. Less is more. A CV is like a rococo building – there is too much to take in — and the wood is obscured by the trees. The second flaw is the emphasis on criteria rather than competencies, which is related to the third flaw: CVs are not customer friendly. Competencies aid the recruitment process. They increase the chance of you being shortlisted. They improve the interview process by examining how you have coped in the past to describe how your experiences can be applied to the future. Competencies increase the likelihood of you being hired as they help unearth what makes you tick and why you are a good fit for the organization. A criteria-based CV therefore needs to be deciphered. Deciphering is an inexact science. You rely on a third party to break the code. Recruitment agencies may get it wrong when making value judgements about you based on less relevant information. They will make these value judgements quickly yet you have provided a catalogue of information that is not focused on their needs.

The CV is under a barrage of consistent attack. However, the biggest force toppling the apparent ubiquity of the CV is the changing corporate landscape.

# criteria are
# but not

## Chopping the corporate structure down to size

The Man from the Pru, the blue-suited IBM sales man and the Japanese salaryman evoke the era of the company man working within a pyramid-shaped, hierarchical organization. These command-and-control structures relied for their success on recruiting specialist functional knowledge into defined silos. There was an emphasis on long-term employment, time in a position was important, knowledge rested within the company and there were clear rules for performance. Careers were essentially vertical as well as defined and delivered through the company.

This organizational structure of time lines, functions and vertical progressions moulded your career. Your CV unsurprisingly mirrors this current organizational structure which in turn mirrors the structure and shape of many recruitment agencies with functional and industry-led silos of 'expertise'. All this changes in a new world of exploding organizational change.

There is a healthy academic debate on the actual breadth, depth and speed of organizational change. This in turn affects career patterns, the nature and scope of management, and the skills and abilities required for the future. However, one thing is not debatable. Change is happening and it has been happening for the last 30 years.

# important
# that important

We are seeing the erosion and breakdown of this predominant corporate hegemony, albeit earlier in some industries than others, coupled with the rise of the 'individual' or 'intelligent' career, in response to a more flexible, decentralized, increasingly virtual, matrix organization. A process that began slowly and predominantly in the early 1970s with the economic slowdown has precipitated into a seismic shift, compounded by the dot.com bubble and reinforced by the recent 21st century global slowdown and the likely impact of technology.

The relevance and usefulness of the command-and-control organization is being challenged. Organizational boundaries are constantly being redrawn in an ebb and flow as organizations seek to drive competitive advantage, manage uncertainty, deliver the promised upside from technology and find their feet in a global economy. The world has been re-engineered, restructured, merged, consolidated, networked, matrixed, downsized and de-layered. Thinner and flatter organizations emerge that lack the formal ties of hierarchy, functional specialists and job titles. New organizational models based on virtual companies with virtual teams, existing only in cyberspace, irrespective

# new-style
# need managers
# capable of learning

of time, space and location, not practicably conceivable several decades ago, could turn into the paradigm of the future.

But let's not get carried away. The world is never an open-and-shut case of black and white. Rather, there are myriad shades of shifting grey. Today, the organizational landscape is littered with varying organizational structures adapting to their market niches. A continuum of organizational structures now exists, sometimes coexisting at the same time, with extremes at either end. We see this range from traditional command-and-control centralized organizations with the emphasis on capital allocation, clear demarcation lines and agreements with other companies, to the flexible, decentralized team-based organizational models emphasizing networked relationships across a flexible matrix with the emphasis on individuals having knowledge, taking action and doing the right thing. However, the fragmentation and erosion of organizational structures changes the way your career will evolve and happen.

These new-style organizations will need managers who are flexible, capable of learning and displaying new skills for the performance of a

**organizations will who are flexible, and displaying new skills**

wide range of changing tasks. Changes in managers' careers therefore come from changes in organizations. This in turn leads to new theories on managerial action, where there is far greater autonomy and fewer directives than in the old bureaucracy. You will need to learn and adapt rather than simply perform and execute. Competencies and internal motivations become more crucial as boundaries evolve.

Iain Herbertson, CEO of Manpower UK, the world's biggest employment agency, put it like this in a recent BBC Radio 4 interview:

**"For everyone to recognize that in today's world all of us need to keep refreshing our skills and picking up training so that we are best equipped, we have transferable skills so that we can take advantage of new work opportunities that occur ... that reflects some of the changes in the employment patterns taking place."**

What you do, when you do it, with whom you work, how you work, and where you do it are all changing into a complex web of multiple relationships. People are now managing their careers actively. Career variety is part and parcel of the career landscape and not necessarily within the same company. Indeed, it is generally accepted that we will now have several careers. Fuzzy and flexible working patterns proliferate, vertical career paths can replace horizontal ones probably crossing lines, project

# Your CV belongs
## obsolete corporate

teams replace functional teams, flexibility and agility are key dynamics, multiple skills are required to navigate around, loyalty to the company declines and the individual owns their career. Specialist knowledge becomes less important than the ability to get things done.

As your career is owned by you and is less dependent on an organization to execute it, you need to ask yourself, 'What drives me? What is my ideal job? Which skills and relationships are most important?' This shift begins with looking at what's available so you can find the job to fit you rather than fit yourself to the job.

As organizational boundaries change, the nature and types of careers that are possible change. As careers change, shouldn't you consider how you sell yourself to make the best opportunity of this new-world paradigm? And, as there is an increasing reliance on individual learning, adaptation and competencies, then surely a criteria-based, functional, linear CV is the wrong document? Your CV belongs to the days of those obsolete corporate monoliths that are crumbling and changing around you.

You need to look at the organizational models of today and see how they are responding to the future. You need to respond and be in tune with the changing workplace.

# to the days of those monoliths that are crumbling

Don't try and solve the issues you have writing a CV as you are correcting a fundamentally flawed document. Rather than focus on criteria and the linear past, you now need to consider your future capability in a non-linear dynamic world and how you prove this to others: this is where the Elevator Pitch comes in.

Welcome to the Elevator Pitch.

chapter

# The birth of the Elevator Pitch

"CVs try to sell, the Elevator Pitch will make employers want to buy."

Charlie Dobres, CEO of i-Level

# The Elevator Pitch who you are and

The Elevator Pitch is the new and improved way to summarize your career and work experience so that better and faster hiring decisions can be made. In this chapter we focus on defining the distinct elements of the Elevator Pitch and in Chapter 3 we will show you how to write your own Elevator Pitch.

A traditional CV emphasizes criteria such as job title to employment history in order to place a value on your career. A CV concentrates on what you are and where you have done it. They are linear static

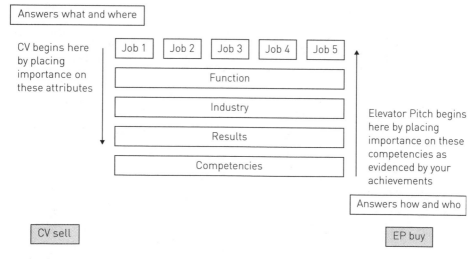

**Figure 2.1**   The correct starting point

# concentrates on why you are who you are

documents written in reverse chronological order. In the last chapter we saw that CVs are fatally flawed. The inherent weakness of your CV restricts your ability to find the best job as the real reason for employing you is hidden. Your information is not correctly prioritized and you fail to answer why you would be a great employee.

On the other hand an Elevator Pitch begins with your behaviours, skills, traits and abilities that define and help predict how you will perform in the future. An Elevator Pitch does not need to be deciphered. Your Elevator Pitch focuses on who you are and how you do it. Your Elevator Pitch is dynamic and non linear. Your Elevator Pitch will be concise, relevant and targeted. Your Elevator Pitch only highlights the information necessary to help you secure your next job allowing your prospective employer to quickly and easily answer the question 'What does this person do or offer me? What is their value add?' This give you a better chance of securing a place on the shortlist and therefore a job.

Figure 2.1 neatly captures this new perspective and starting point: the correct starting point of an Elevator Pitch and the wrong starting point of a CV.

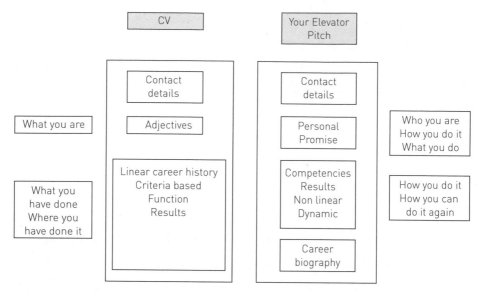

**Figure 2.2** Highlighting the big difference

There are four core elements to your Elevator Pitch,

➡ Personal details. Name, contact details including your e-mail address and international dialling codes.

➡ Your Personal Promise. Think of this as your own executive summary, based on the three core components of who you are, how you do it and what you do.

➡ Your Transferable Assets. These are your competencies, behaviours, traits and abilities that are relevant to the job you are

# Competencies themselves in you

applying for. Your achievements are used as evidence of your skill in that particular competency

➡ Short career biography. A list of the companies you have worked for, positions held and length of service.

Figure 2.2 shows the differences between a CV and your Elevator Pitch.

## The Personal Promise

The Personal Promise is your executive summary. It replaces the list of unstructured adjectives that many people include on a CV. If you have ever reviewed several CVs, these adjectives become meaningless as everyone uses stock phrases. Your Personal Promise has three key components.

➡ Who you are

➡ How you do it

➡ What you do

In Chapter 5, you will find a number of Elevator Pitches. From these, two Personal Promises have been highlighted as they provide good examples of tackling the three components in a couple of sentences.

**"I bring zest for life to my work making ideas happen. 14 years of practical, integrated marketing ideas generation for both clients and advertising agencies across the world."**

# manifest
# and are hard
# to imitate

**"Customer-focused, intelligent risk taker. Direction setter of inventive solutions with the willingness to absorb situations and get on with it. 28 years' leadership of multimillion-dollar mechanical engineering projects in the international oil industry."**

The Personal Promise is similar to a strapline in a magazine: easy to take in and very easily understood. The Personal Promise sets the tone and style of the Elevator Pitch. It is an umbrella statement that the rest of your Elevator Pitch sets out to prove.

## Transferable Assets

Transferable Assets are your fiduciary currency. Just as a bank note promises to pay the bearer a certain sum in the future, your Transferable Assets are your tokens that guarantee the promise of your future contribution and value.

A Transferable Asset is a competency that you are skilled in. A competency is what you are good at. More importantly, they are what you are better at than other people, so they have a degree of relative and absolute measure. A competency is one aspect of your make-up, your underlying motives and traits that differentiate outstanding from typical performance. Competencies give you a source of differentiation and generate distinct value and benefits. Competencies manifest themselves in you and are hard to imitate.

Competencies focus on how you do a job and the way you do it rather than what you do. They describe the underlying characteristics that enable you to perform better in your role and go beyond the traditional focus of your qualifications, technical skills and experience. Competencies are observable and measurable. Some competencies are easy to pick up, while others are difficult to learn and some cannot be acquired.

The key is to discover the ones you have, the ones that you are developing, and the ones that are sitting on the horizon. In this way, you will see the progression of the early behaviours that form a competency.

To understand and get to grips with your Transferable Assets you need to quantify their quality. This quantification process can be absolute, relative or perceived. It also needs to be objective and ideally benchmarked against norms. In Chapter 3, we show you in detail how to define your own Transferable Assets.

You can also be skilled, unskilled or overskilled in your use of each competency. The word 'skill' refers to your degree of ability or capability. If you have demonstrated a competency just once, then it is unlikely that you are skilled in that area, so you cannot claim it is one of your Transferable Assets. Conversely, one can become overskilled or over-reliant in the use of one competency, which negates the upside of using the competency.

We can merely scratch the surface of competencies in this book. There is a wealth of data on competencies. If you type the word 'competency' into a good search engine, you'll find hundreds and thousands of references. Hay McBer and Lominger are the leaders of this field and their websites are good starting points: **www.lominger.com**; **www.haygroup.com**. Happy hunting.

Your Transferable Assets define you. They are you. They are your essential building blocks. Your Transferable Assets form your Career DNA.

## Career DNA

Your Career DNA sets you apart from all other individuals and gives you your own Career DNA fingerprint that is easily identifiable. However, unlike biological DNA, your Career DNA expands as you experience new roles, dynamics, cultures, events and tasks within the workplace and social environment.

When constructing your Elevator Pitch you need to pick and select the relevant and most pertinent Transferable Assets to suit the project you're facing. This is fairly similar to your own biological DNA, when certain parts of the genetic code are switched on and other parts switched off to form specialized cells most suited to the task in hand.

Competencies also help you understand the type of organization and culture where you thrive best as a company's culture is defined by the people it employs.

Through placing emphasis on competencies, you redress the recruitment balance (Figures 2.3 and 2.4).

The Elevator Pitch reverses the CV (Figure 2.5).

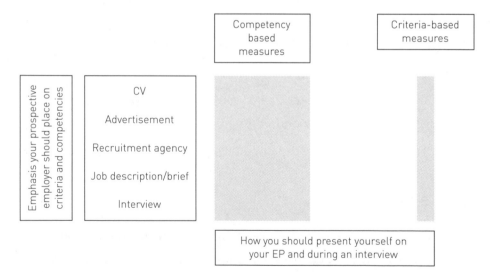

**Figure 2.3**  The Elevator Pitch redresses the balance

| Executive summary | Transferable Asset | Results | Job | Industry sector | Career history |
|---|---|---|---|---|---|
| Your Personal Promise | Transferable Asset 1 | Results A<br>Results B | Job 4<br>Job 3 | Industry B<br>Industry B | |
| | Transferable Asset 2 | Results C<br>Results D | Job 3<br>Job 2 | Industry B<br>Industry A | Chronological job history |
| | Transferable Asset 3 | Results E<br>Results F | Job 4<br>Job 4 | Industry B<br>Industry B | Functional growth |
| | Transferable Asset 4 | Results G<br>Results H | | | |

← Hierarchy of emphasis of what you expose to the world

**Figure 2.4**   The Elevator Pitch framework

Hierarchy of emphasis of what you expose to the world

←————————————————————————|————————————————————————→

Your fundamental building blocks
Who you are
Why you are who you are
How you do it
Why you can do it again

Functional, criteria-led, linear catalogue
What you are
Where you have been
What you have done

**Figure 2.5**   The brilliant Elevator Pitch principle

# The Career DNA Bank

You will discover you have many Transferable Assets. You will use a selection of your Transferable Assets on each Elevator Pitch you write. You need a quick and easy way to refer to your Transferable Assets so you can pick and choose the best ones for the job you are applying for. We have called this your Career DNA Bank.

Essentially you should think of your Career DNA Bank as a toolkit. A Career DNA Bank is a repository of your Transferable Assets. These Transferable Assets can be either deposited or withdrawn at will to target a specific industry or role fully maximizing your potential.

A Career DNA Bank is good allowing you to make bespoke Elevator Pitches. How often have you done this in the past with your CV? Not much is our guess, as the level of tailoring is pretty limited with a time-line, criteria-based CV. However Transferable Assets can be presented in a much more dynamic and fluid manner adjusting to your needs. The results-driven evidence that supports each Transferable Asset can be displayed in a number of ways and different evidence can be used to support variations in the overall Transferable Asset.

Transferable Assets can be grouped into four clusters: job-specific, people-specific, function-specific and behaviour-specific assets (Figure 2.6).

| | Competencies | Examples |
|---|---|---|
| **Your Career DNA Bank** | People-specific | Works the matrix, persuasive, inspirational manager, cares about direct reports |
| | Job-specific | Understands role within organization, robust analytical skills, customer segmentation, articulate spokesperson, works hard, plays hard |
| | Function-specific | Understands what goes on around the organization, fiscally, legally, operations, external ventures |
| | Behaviour-specific | Emotional IQ, sets correct targets, results-driven, long-range thinking, stands alone and challenges convention, intellectually sharp and agile, picks up concepts easily |

**Figure 2.6**   Your Career DNA Bank

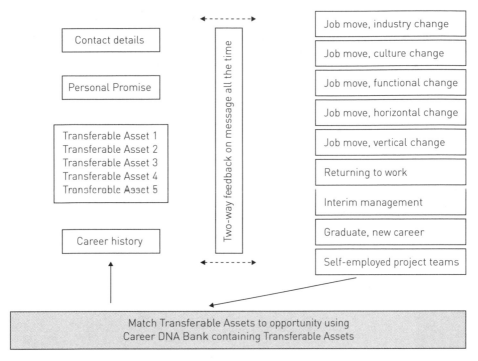

**Figure 2.7**  Mud thrown is lost ground – the importance of the message

Figure 2.7 shows the elements of an Elevator Pitch.

The Elevator Pitch aids dialogue and encourages communication in a common and universally recognized language that is used by your customers. There is no need to decipher the information as a common bond is established. The Elevator Pitch is highly adaptable.

Your Elevator Pitch helps you get the job you want.

chapter

# 3

# Writing your Elevator Pitch

To write your own Elevator Pitch, you must first consider each element.

There are four core elements to your Elevator Pitch,

→ Personal details: name and contact details, including your email address and international dialling code. This is self-explanatory.

→ Your Personal Promise, based on the three core components of who you are, how you do it, and what you do.

→ Your Transferable Assets, chosen from your Career DNA Bank justified by the use of results, which we call quantifying the quality.

→ Short career biography, stating the companies you have worked for, positions held, and length of service.

The Elevator Pitch should reflect the needs of your audience. We know they are looking for concise, relevant, targeted and pertinent information. We also know they don't have a lot of time. Help them, because you will be helping yourself. Write a short Elevator Pitch. If you cannot write your Elevator Pitch on one page, why not rethink what you are writing? If it is more than two pages long, you are definitely not being hard enough on yourself.

# The Elevator Pitch
## the needs of

## Your Personal Promise

Your Personal Promise is your executive summary. It is you in a nutshell. How do you crack it? All Personal Promises are founded on three component questions:

➡ Who you are?

➡ How you do it?

➡ What you do?

Before we learn how to write your own Personal Promise, let's consider two we have already seen in Chapter 2 and pull them apart.

Bill's Personal Promise is: 'I bring zest for life to my work, making ideas happen. 14 years of practical, integrated marketing ideas generation for both clients and advertising agencies across the world.'

John's Personal Promise is: 'Customer focused, intelligent risk taker. Direction setter of inventive solutions with the willingness to absorb situations and get on with it. 28 years' leadership of $ multimillion mechanical engineering projects in the international oil industry.'

# should reflect
# your audience

# Your Personal
# be direct,

The 'Who you are?' component is answered by 'I bring zest for life to my work' and 'Customer-focused, intelligent risk taker'. What does this tell you about these two people? One has a sense of fun and passion, and plays hard and works hard, in a larger-than-life outgoing capacity. The second person is more contained, in a balanced practical manner, and relishes challenges and the associated risk. John is passionate about his customers and what they want yet he is willing to make that big leap through quantifying the risk.

The second component is 'How you do it?' This is a summation of your overall competencies at a broad level. Here, we have 'Making ideas happen [through the zest for life]' and 'Direction setter of inventive solutions with the willingness to absorb situations and get on with it'. What underpins these statements? In order to make things happen, Bill challenges the way things are done, asks whether they can be done better and doesn't just think about an idea but acts upon it and gets stuck in. John's statement shows he is a man who is comfortable and content in fluid situations requiring flexibility of mind, balanced by the ability to juggle many balls simultaneously. During all of this he inspires confidence in his team coupled with the ability to cut to the main issue and assess what is important, why it is important and how

# Promise should simple, clear **and directional**

it should be tackled, sometimes in an unorthodox yet highly practical and pragmatic manner.

The third question that needs answering is, 'What do you do?' This is the only part of the Elevator Pitch that is criteria-based with a linear, functional perspective. It provides the support for the two previous questions. Both have tackled this by showing the length of time, industry sector and geographical regions where they have worked: '14 years of practical, integrated marketing ideas generation for both clients and advertising agencies across the world' and '28 years leadership of $ multimillion mechanical engineering projects in the international oil industry'.

Your Personal Promise should be direct, simple, clear and directional. It should be you. There should be a part of you in the Personal Promise that your friends could spot. It is the umbrella statement that sets out your stall, which your Transferable Assets then support. The Personal Promise is the conductor and your Transferable Assets are the orchestra. The Personal Promise is your sound bite.

We would expect to see further evidence that proves these statements in their full Elevator Pitches.

Seems easy enough doesn't it, but let's start in another industry.

We've all heard that movies are pitched to studios. Budding writers toil over a story, craft a synopsis, and then ruthlessly simplify it down to a core sound bite. The sound bite for Alien was allegedly 'Jaws in Space'.

This sound bite is known as a positioning statement. Positioning was first defined by Ries and Trout in the early 1970s and has become the underpinning of the marketing world over the last 30 years. Many people talk positioning. But few really do it. The fundamental premise is to concentrate on the relationships in your customers' minds and reconnect them in new and exciting ways. That's why 'Jaws in Space' works so well.

Everybody, unconsciously or consciously, practises rudimentary positioning. Positioning is a prerequisite for selective communication. How many messages do you receive in any one day? Not just commercial messages, such as advertising hoardings or television commercials, but what about that selective political sound bite on international or domestic affairs? Was it the whole truth? Of course not. We don't have the time or the space in our heads for the whole truth. Selective communication reigns supreme in our 24/7 world. Global companies such as Unilever or Shell practise positioning to find angles for their products. Countries do it to encourage tourism. Cities

## does your

do it. People do it. It is an angle. It is selective communication, not all-encompassing communication.

When you become selective in your approach to communication you must ask yourself what particular aspect you wish to showcase and what would help your customers buy from you.

It's excellent practice to play with pitching your favourite movie, book or play in this way so that when it comes to you the whole process will become much easier. You'll then find it easier to be ruthlessly selective and to focus only on your advantages and benefits.

What's your sound bite? What's your Personal Promise? You may have 30 seconds to convince someone to hire you. Or you may get 2 minutes or 10. Don't they say first impressions count? What do you say?

Why not write it down? Did you think like your CV – straitjacketed into convention? What did you leave out? Why? What was your focus on? Was it chronological? Autobiographical? Perhaps functional? Did you refer to things you had done and achieved in the past? Or did you focus on how you might be described by your partner? Was it a linear view? Perhaps you outlined several objective–analysis–action–result-style scenarios. Did you emphasize the blue-chip nature of your career to date? Or did you focus on the bigger picture? Perhaps you highlighted the boldness of your entrepreneurial stance in a task-driven culture. Or

# Personal Promise
## sell you?

maybe your personal capital. You undoubtedly looked into your past career and highlighted a couple of facets that you felt proud of.

If a sound bite can sell a movie, does your Personal Promise sell you? Does your Personal Promise cover the three bases?

➡ Who you are?

➡ How you do it?

➡ What you do?

The first component, 'Who you are?', is best answered by thinking of examples from other fields and then applying these to yourself. If you were to describe your best friend, how would you describe them? You'd probably focus on a string of adjectives that bring their personality to life rather than their physical description. It's simple to describe your friends. What would they say about you? Go and grab your favourite author. How have they described their characters and places? There is probably some haunting description you read months ago that lurks in your mind as a powerful evocation of someone's intent. What is yours? How does this translate into your work experience?

To answer the second question, 'How you do it?', you need to think about why someone is better than someone else, and then apply this to yourself. What makes for a great doctor rather than a mediocre doctor? Is it the number of patients they can see in a day, or is it the reassurance and self-confidence of their bedside manner, their compassion, or the way they make bad news sound just that bit better? Think about some of your previous bosses. What made one better than the other? What distinguished their performance? Did they focus solely on the end result and nothing about the means? Or did they create strong morale and spirit in their team? Were the wins and successes shared? Did they create a feeling of belonging? Did they provide challenging and stretching tasks? Were they dedicated to their customers? Did they quickly zero in on the essential items and create focus? Did you admire their inspirational leadership qualities? Were they a doer? Did the impossible happen? Similarly, going back in time, you probably respected and responded better to some teachers than others. Which teachers do you still think about, and why? Did they involve you? Were the lessons fun? Why were they fun? What did they do to make them fun? Did they root a theoretical subject in the everyday here and now? Did they pass on a burning passion for their subject and make you want to find out more? Did you gaze at the night sky after a physics lesson and dream about the enormity of the universe? What are the overall patterns of behaviour that you have? Quite simply, how do you do things? What's your fire?

The third part of the Personal Promise is linear and criteria-based. This is a summary of your experience, the industry sector or sectors, your profession and perhaps geographical location.

Figure 3.1 summarizes the types of question that you may find useful in creating your Personal Promise.

You do not need to have just one Personal Promise. There will be times when you wish to portray slightly different aspects of your character. Once you have created your first Personal Promise, try and look at yourself from different angles and see other facets that might be useful.

However, to write your Personal Promise, and to produce the perfect set-up for your Elevator Pitch, you need to create your Transferable Assets and populate your Career DNA Bank.

| Who you are? | How do your friends describe you? <br> How would your favourite author describe you? <br> What's your strapline? <br> What would a TV ad for you say? |
|---|---|
| How you do it? | What makes a teacher a good teacher? <br> What makes a doctor a good doctor? <br> What makes a boss a good boss? <br> What makes you a good employee/ <br> employer/interim manager? |
| What you do? | Number of years worked <br> Industry sector <br> Profession and geographical location |

**Figure 3.1** The Personal Promise

## Defining your Transferable Assets

You now need to populate your Career DNA Bank with your Transferable Assets and the evidence that can be used as substantiation.

There are four basic steps in identifying and evidencing your Transferable Assets:

1. Look back on your career and deconstruct it project by project, thinking about each objective, your analysis, the resulting action, and the end result.

2. Understand what the objectives, analysis, actions and results tell you about your behaviours and motives.

**try and look at different**

3. Create your Transferable Assets by looking at the behaviours and competencies you can support.

4. Create your Career DNA Bank.

**Step 1** **Deconstructing your career**

To begin this process, you need to take a thorough look back through your career, concentrating on those situations where you have been highly successful. You should consider not only the macro-objectives, such as a 10% growth in profit margin year on year, but also the micro-objectives behind this that led you to achieving that growth.

You may have already done some of this work for your appraisals and in constructing your original CV. One of the tools you may find useful is the objectives–analysis–action–results (OAAR) approach. This is a fairly standard approach to quantifying results within given parameters:

➡ What were the objectives?

➡ What analysis did you make?

➡ What action did you take?

➡ What were the results?

# yourself from angles

Here is an example of a top-line OAAR study from a veterinary nurse:

**Objective:** To lead and ensure the smooth running of a team of seven nurses in a busy mixed country practice.

**Analysis:** Benchmark similar practices around the country. Looked at previous two years' vet practice management (who does what, where, when, why). Found seasonal trend.

**Action:** Developed new staff rotas. Created optimal business mix, freed up additional 20 hours a month of time for every four employees.

**Results:** An efficient practice where vets could be vets. Ensured nursing staff were available for theatre, consulting, laboratory, hospitalized patients, practice administration including small-animal claim forms, nursing rotas, and on-call out-of-hour duties. Made time available for practice nurses and resources for the dispensing of drugs and the teaching of student nurses.

However, the really important information can be found behind the smaller steps you took in order to deliver the whole objective. Did you need to manage your team in a different manner or reorganize it? What

# really important found behind the

processes and procedures did you need? How did you manage the learning requirements of your team? Was there a new business win that drove margins higher but required greater relationship skills? You should then reanalyze each of these micro-objectives and ask yourself what you did, how you did it, and why you did it. Again, you may find you need to be even more granular and repeat the process again and again. It may help you to think of this whole exercise as a Russian doll: opening one doll reveals the next, opening that doll reveals the next, and so on. Each new doll exposed takes you deeper into your analysis and actions, which constitute how you delivered the larger objective.

On the surface you may find that answering these questions is a simple and straightforward affair. However, peeling back the layers to get under your skin can be trickier than it looks. Here are some questions that might help:

⇒ How did you arrive at the objectives?

⇒ What skills did you use to analyse the project?

⇒ How did you go about implementing the objectives and analysis?

⇒ How were the results derived?

⇒ What did you actually do to solve the problem?

# information can be smaller steps you took

➡ How did others contribute?

➡ How were resources managed?

➡ How did you formulate the answer?

➡ What barriers did you encounter?

➡ How did they affect the project?

➡ What made the difference?

➡ What were the organizational factors?

➡ Which behaviours worked, and why?

Probably the easiest way to do this exercise is to write a narrative story. Get everything down. Then rewrite it several times until you reach a logical, neat story. Here is an example from Michael's experiences at Dell:

Whilst working for the European head office of Dell Computers I was tasked with delivering and running the new corporate brand advertising campaign across Europe and so effect changes in Dell's brand equity. This involved planning and buying print and television media across several European countries, as well as adapting our television commercials, which had been shot in both the USA and Europe, for a European audience.

However, there was one small problem. Television advertising is expensive. It is especially expensive when buying commercials in pro-grammes that attract a business audience such as news and current affairs. I had to ensure I invested the media budget wisely and effectively to deliver our objectives. Germany, in particular, was in need of extra help. It was a key strategic sales geography as well as being the largest European IT market so we needed to provide a sustained and enhanced campaign without compromising our other markets. There was not enough money to do this.

When budgets and objectives don't square, you have two choices: change the objective or change the budget. You also have a third choice: change the budget without actually changing the budget.

The campaign was launched with a budget nearly 50% greater than originally planned. This allowed Dell to dramatically increase the campaign's reach and effectiveness and allowed us to fully support each business and especially support the German market over a period of one year. However, this budget increase was achieved without needing extra cash.

The 'zero cost incremental budget' was delivered through a series of innovative, symbiotic, back-to-back deals with a range of partners covering the worlds of media, sport and IT. It proved conclusively that there is such a thing as a free lunch. The astonishing net result was the delivery of one year's free airtime on two German television stations on top of the already planned media, as well as Dell becoming the primary sponsor of the newly minted Williams BMW 1999 Le Mans Racing Team, again for nothing.

For those racing fanatics, 1999 was the year that Williams BMW won Le Mans. Suddenly, our primary sponsorship of a racing car reaped the additional benefits of a free global sponsorship property. This covered major worldwide television coverage during the race through to BMW's advertising across the world announcing their win. Naturally, the Dell logo was always visible and shining bright. Model cars were sent to our customers. Books were published with tailored dust jackets. The win was also used in Dell's own direct-response advertising to convey leadership. Employees were excited and it became the highest visited page within the European Dell internal newsletter hosted on our intranet.

# How do

A major success that began by looking at how to increase budgets without extra cash and ended with a highly visible global sponsorship project and a robust year-long media campaign in Germany.

You may find it helpful to transfer the key learnings to a simple OAAR table. Naturally, you will find that for each area, you will be writing several different OAAR scripts as the layers are pulled back and exposed.

**Step 2** **Understanding what the analysis, action and results tell you – who you are, how you did it, what you did, and where you did it**

Once you have constructed your basic story outlines, you need to analyze what each part actually means. The objective provides the context to the problem or opportunity. The analysis and action sections provide the clues to your behaviour patterns. These two key sections answer the question, 'How do you do things?' The end result answers what you did. In the future months and years, you would not be seeking to replicate the result, but you would be seeking to use the behaviours underlying your analysis and action, and applying these to new opportunities and problems. This is shown in Figure 3.2.

Referring back to the case study of Michael at Dell, we can see how he has analyzed what he did and what behaviours he demonstrated. What were the motives, traits and behaviour patterns that made

# you
# do things?

him successful in delivering the outcome required and distinguished excellent performance from average performance?

The overall objective was to deliver a change in Dell's brand equity through running a corporate television campaign across Europe. The first analysis found that the objectives and budgets were incompatible. This created a new micro-objective to leverage the existing funds and make them go further. The analysis was to create a step change in the budget by looking outside the normal funding arena and developing new models of participation. The action was a series of lateral, creative, symbiotic and interlinking partnerships with companies inside and outside the IT arena. The result was a 50% increase in budget without any cost to Dell, as well as the creation of a free global sponsorship property.

| | Provides | Implication |
|---|---|---|
| Objective | Context | Benchmark |
| Analysis | How you do it<br>Who you are | You can do it again |
| Action | How you do it<br>Who you are | You can do it again |
| Results | What you do | History |

**Figure 3.2** Key performance indicators

There's a bias for action and results. There is a thirst for tough and unfamiliar challenges coupled with the desire and need to seize an opportunity. It incorporates a commercial knowledge and cultural understanding of the business. It shouts loudly about his creativity and freshness of thinking, showing an intellectually agile mind capable of juggling concepts and complexity. A tenacity to break the mould, to experiment, and to not accept the status quo is clearly defined. Good-quality decisions were made under extreme time pressures, often without all the data. And there is a clear creative edge to solving problems and seeing patterns where none existed previously.

On top of these behaviours, Michael also relied on his 15 years of advertising and marketing knowledge to help ground his actions and break down the desired outcome into smaller chunks.

There are many facets to a work project of this nature. There are many desired outcomes, and many OAARs can be built. For example, one starting point for analysis could be the actual changes in brand equity. Another could be how well the agencies were managed and the subsequent media planning and buying performance. Each of these stories would emphasize a set of behaviours that could be drawn upon in different ways.

Here is another example, from Bill, illustrating the analysis of one part of the role he played in winning new business for his company.

Whilst working in Australia for a top advertising agency, I was responsible for generating new business opportunities. A newspaper group came to us with a fascinating dilemma. How could we help them strengthen their customer service by improving the relationship between their salesforce and their client counterparts whilst driving efficiencies by providing accurate up-to-the-minute information regardless of the Australian time zones? My task was to win the business.

We identified a number of new customers alongside those identified in their original brief. We created interlinked intranet, internet and extranet sites sharing common data that provided customized information to each audience. This allowed their sales teams to be fully up to date whenever and wherever they were providing enhanced client service. For their clients, it delivered a greater speed of response.

I had to manage teams, marshal resources, gain direction and buy-in, set priorities, understand the commercial imperatives of their business, step back and see the wider context and the big picture.

Each story and each OAAR set helps you understand your behaviours, base traits and motives. Following is a list of some of the themes and behaviours that could underlie some of your Transferable Assets. It is by no means exhaustive, but should be used merely to get you thinking about how you might describe how you behave. Think back to the type of interview questions you have been asked. There are some classic questions, such as, 'Have you led a team during a crisis? How did this compare with calmer times?' or 'Tell me about a time you had to deal with conflict.' Think of all the questions that tried to get under your skin and highlight the behaviours you have. Write down these questions. Write down the questions you ask others. Look for the groups of behaviours. Think about how you might respond. Go back to your OAAR analysis. Look for commonly used threads:

- Good negotiator
- Provides perspective
- Sees patterns and trends
- Customer-focused
- Flexibility and adaptability
- Copes with the unexpected
- Moves on and is not phased
- Intellectual agility
- Inclusive and collaborative across the matrix
- Green-fielding
- It ain't what you do, it's the way that you do it
- Passionate
- Deals with imprecision
- Helps others succeed
- Resourceful
- Rigorous strategic thinker
- Works through others to deliver objectives
- Commercial awareness
- Creativity and innovation
- Lateral thinker

- Committed
- Solid business strategist
- Resource- and team-management
- Plain speaker
- Motivational leader
- Provides practical business solutions
- Results-driven
- Business builder
- Understands people
- Business development
- Consistent
- Information gathering
- Situational awareness
- Effective communicator
- Technical and practical aptitude
- Building great teams
- Relationship and partnership building
- Challenges convention
- Sales development

- Ability to influence
- Problem solver
- Motivates others
- Cares for people
- Managing and measuring
- Decision making
- Managing through systems
- Planning
- Stands alone
- Thrives on challenges
- Facilitates organizational success
- Forward thinking
- Identify viable business Opportunities
- Intellectual power
- Rational yet analytical enquiring mind
- Long-range thinker
- Cuts to the core of what is required
- Identifies priority actions
- Gives others scope and

- freedom to act
- Discovers concepts, trends and patterns
- Draws inferences
- Abstract reasoning
- Verbal reasoning
- Tenacity to deliver
- Tenacity to break the mould
- Driven style
- Principled
- Integrity and trust
- Honesty
- Loyal
- Intellectual breadth and depth
- Sets priorities
- Comfortably handles risk and uncertainty
- Can shift gears
- Mentoring
- Understands and uses the informal network to get things done

### Step 3  Allocating a skill level to each of your identified competencies creates your Transferable Assets

A Transferable Asset is a competency or behaviour that you are skilled in. How do you determine the skill level you attribute to a competence? This depends on a number of things.

It could be the number of times it has been used; you can check this by looking at the frequency at which the same type of behaviour or group of behaviours crops up in your analyses of projects. It might help you to construct a table like that shown in Figure 3.3.

| | Your story | Behaviours displayed | Arranged into groups |
|---|---|---|---|
| Objective | | | |
| Analysis | | | |
| Action | | | |
| Results | | | |

**Figure 3.3**  Key performance indicators

# Superficiality

How effective have you been in using the competence and to what extent has it influenced the outcome of projects? These can be used as major indicators as to whether this competence is a real strength.

The acid test is how many concrete examples you can provide. If you claim to be innovative, then you will need several examples to prove it. The proof is not just the examples you write for your Elevator Pitch. These are meant to be the best examples that you would prioritize over others and talk about first. What would happen if you were asked for another example of this style of behaviour? And another? And another? You need to be able to drill down and provide the depth and breadth of your skills and abilities in this area. Superficiality counts for nothing. Not everyone is results-driven. Not everyone is innovative. Not everyone is creative. What are you?

Look back at your OAAR tables. Do you see common patterns? What behaviours do you display?

## Step 4 Creating your Career DNA Bank

Your Career DNA is stored in a Career DNA Bank. Think of this as a deposit account. Identifying all your Transferable Assets at the outset ensures you have a full bank account with a rich currency reserve. Many of us have numerous Transferable Assets, all of which are

# counts for
# nothing

relevant. Just not all at the same time. Some have been built up, while others are being nurtured and progressed. This is an ongoing process throughout your whole career.

You have identified consistently used behaviour patterns. These need to be written up ready for use in your Elevator Pitches.

John Baldwin has identified his Transferable Assets using the processes described and built his own Career DNA Bank. He has used a three-step process to write and explain his Transferable Assets that are going to be used in his Elevator Pitch:

**Step 1:** Decide what key words best describe your Transferable Assets in a positive and realistic way. You are looking to impress upon the reader that you are the right person for the role, so choose your words carefully. It is imperative that the style and tone of your Transferable Assets reflect you and evidences your Personal Promise. It is worth reminding yourself at this stage of phrases that would be considered as negative and would create unfavourable impressions. It is a sure-fire way of making sure you don't use them by mistake. John initially created the table shown in Figure 3.4.

**Step 2:** You have selected key descriptive words and/or phrases to help build and evidence your Transferable Assets. Now you need to look at those parts of your career that evidence your Transferable Assets and, most importantly, you wish to highlight. Your Transferable Assets were defined previously by using the detailed OAAR analysis technique. For each of the Transferable Assets that you have chosen to use on your Elevator Pitch there will be many parts of your career that you can use to highlight them. List these as shown in Figure 3.5.

| Categories | Positive keywords for Elevator Pitch | Negative words or impressions to be avoided |
|---|---|---|
| People | Supportive, encouraging, guiding, mentor, even-handed, fair and reasonable, sincere, approachable, flexible | Cautious, conservative, reserved |
| Job | Analytical, articulate, inventive, thinks outside the box, co-ordinated, disciplined, organized, vocal participant, prudent, leader, communicator, direction setter | Observer, quiet, follower, indecisive |
| Functional | Product knowledge, hands-on, international, cultural awareness, new business ventures, JVs, agents, key accounts, externally focused, fiscal awareness, contract awareness, terms and condtions, legal entity | Inexperience, parochial, tunnel vision |
| Behaviour | Positive, flexible, intelligent risk taker, lateral mover, social, languages, flexible | Negative, dour, inflexible, outrageous, prejudiced |

**Figure 3.4**   John Baldwin's Career DNA Bank

| Categories | Transferable assets | Notes |
|---|---|---|
| People | Supportive, approachable, fair and reasonable | For use in describing my HR-associated role in expat job |
| Job | Analytical, communication | Reference my engineering background |
| Functional | Hands-on, outside the box | My industry experience |
| Behaviour | Lateral mover, flexibility | My willingness to absorb situations and get on with it |
| | | All resulting in enhanced business results |

**Figure 3.5**   Transferable Asset Analyser

**Step 3:** You have now selected your Transferable Assets with notes attached showing how they evidence your career. You need to combine these to build them up using your actual experiences to create a fully evidenced Transferable Asset. Remember not to use industry jargon or abbreviations. You are setting out your stall and are aiming to make a real and excellent first impression. You now have a rich currency reserve in your Career DNA Bank. Let's spend it. Your Transferable Assets are now in a format that are ready to use when creating your Elevator Pitch. (Figure 3.6).

| Fair and reasonable, supportive, approachable | I managed 12 expatriate employees in three Middle Eastern countries, most of whom were family accompanied. I had responsibility for the equitable administration of company policy in areas such as housing, local benefits, schooling, vehicles, home leaves, etc., requiring a fair and reasonable approach with even-handed treatment for all. Living conditions in the late 1970s were trying and required a supportive and approachavble management style. |
|---|---|
| Analytical, communication | My engineering background gives me an analytical nature and as GM and VP, I chaired weekly production meetings and successfully analysed critical path processes to keep delivery schedules on track through the disruptive period of a plant-expansion programme.<br><br>Participation in major tender authorship together with personal presentations to key account clients using communication skills dramatically improved bid package content and contributed to four new account and territory successes in a two-year period while maintaining all existing accounts. |
| Hands-on, outside the box | Eight years in field service management in international offshore and onshore operations have given me a sound hands-on industry competence. (GM Kvaerner Oilfield Prducts – Middle East)<br><br>Instigated and set up a unique JV manufacturing partnership in Iran resulting in a market entry over a four-year period generating sales revenue of $5m. This continues to develop and grow. This was very much an 'outside the box' strategy not initially considered workable by some. |
| Lateral mover, flexibility | Accepted a lateral move as a career-development opportunity and a chance to develop from scratch a complete sales and marketing presence where none had existed. This resulted in sales exceeding $5m/annum within two years and a threefold increase in head count plus an additional district office set-up.<br><br>I am a well-rounded individual having demonstrated a flexibilty that has progressed me through 10 senior positions, in 10 postings (six international) with three multinational companies that have required a solid mix of business and pleasure with colleagues and clients. Throughout I have been ably encouraged by a supportive wife and family. |

**Figure 3.6**   Squaring the circle on your transferable assets

## Critiquing your Elevator Pitch

Your CV described what you did. Your Elevator Pitch describes who you are, your behaviours, your characteristics, and how you do what you do. Your Elevator Pitch should have a resonance about it. You should be able to recognize you. The Elevator Pitch is a mirror. If your reflection is cloudy, you'll need to rethink your words and actions.

Easy to say, hard to do. Start by revisiting your Personal Promise and ask the three questions of yourself again. Who are you? How do you do it? What do you do? Ask a good friend or colleague to look through it. Are they looking at a picture of you that they recognize to be true? Can they see you?

If your Personal Promise changes, then you may need to revisit some of the Transferable Assets and decide whether they evidence your amended Personal Promise.

You will instinctively know when it is right, as you will see you, and your colleagues or friends will be able to confirm this easily.

chapter

# The benefits of the Elevator Pitch

"Today's business goals are being moved at ever-increasing speeds. It therefore matters less what you have done and more what you can do. The Elevator Pitch addresses this head on."

Mark Baldry, Managing Director of Infoline Conferences Ltd

The recent dot.com bubble heralded a change in the recruitment process. People were recruited on the basis of their behaviours and competencies irrespective of function and industry. This created some fabulous teams of like-minded people from diverse backgrounds united by a hunger and passion to change the world. They worked hard. They played hard. They were bright and articulate. Many of you joined the gold rush. Many column inches have been written about the Internet crash. Sure, many companies had no solid business models, but the reality is that the Internet is only just beginning to change the world – but this is obscured by the negative publicity. It would be nice if another legacy was a more enduring contribution to the way we recruit people. Perhaps those who joined dot.com companies will, in turn, never forget the spark that came from having such a diverse group of talented people.

The Elevator Pitch is all about the feelings and associations that create the need for you so buyers will buy. This is in stark contrast to the old CV model that can be characterized as the interrupt–repeat model of communication, where the buyer is not really brought into the buying process. The Elevator Pitch changes seller push into buyer pull.

Probably the best way to look at the Elevator Pitch is to think about how the Elevator Pitch would present itself.

# The Elevator Pitch
## push into

The Personal Promise would be about directness in solving a particular issue. It would probably say:

**"I am direct, focused, forthright. I am mad about my customers. I focus on competencies and behaviour patterns rather than criteria to make the distinction between who you are and how you do it, not what you are and where you have done it. I offer a compelling analytical process that improves recruitment processes and meets the needs of today's career landscape."**

## Flexibility and adaptability

**Objective:** Bespoke sales tool easily refined and defined for each task.

**Analysis:** Understanding and breaking down the position and analyzing your Career DNA to successfully construct your approach.

**Action:** The correct selection of your Personal Promise and Transferable Assets combined with results that evidence them.

**Result:** A targeted and focused personal sales strategy.

# changes seller
# buyer pull

## Forward looking

**Objective:** Concentrates on your future potential, not your historical past.

**Analysis:** You debunk your CV of its historical and linear façade.

**Action:** Creation of Career DNA Bank.

**Result:** Concise understanding of your capabilities and how these match with future jobs.

## Establishing rapport

**Objective:** Establish and use the universal language of behaviours and competencies.

**Analysis:** You identify your Transferable Assets.

**Action:** Concise, tailored, relevant, pertinent information is provided for position you apply for.

**Result:** Quickly establishes 'what does this person do or offer me? What is their value add?' Maximizes opportunity to hire. Begin recruitment process from correct viewpoint. Better selection and hiring process.

# The Elevator Pitch
# where

## Results-driven

**Objective:** To create the need for you.

**Analysis:** Match your Transferable Assets to the role.

**Action:** Effective use of Transferable Assets.

**Results:** The buyer wants to buy you.

The Elevator Pitch helps you go where you want to go. Lord Norman Tebbit, a former UK cabinet minister, used the phrase 'Get on your bike' in the early 1980s to encourage us to think about change, relocate, further our education and professional skills, and to think about how we could grow intellectually. The Elevator Pitch is a physical demonstration of the tangible and intangible attributes of Norman's bike.

There are numerous career changes you can make, and they could take many different forms (Figure 4.1).

You make the new opportunities. The Elevator Pitch merely frames them. This makes it possible to move more easily across industry boundaries, through cultural boundaries, across country divides, and from one job function to another. This is in perfect harmony with the changing career landscape.

helps you go
you want to go

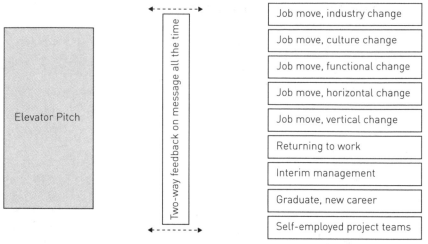

**Figure 4.1** Where are you going

These possibilities can be summarized by the acronym, CLLIF (culture, language, location, industry, function):

*Culture:* company culture, industry culture, social culture.
*Language:* change of language, say English to Spanish or German.
*Location:* relocating geographically, within the same country or crossing international borders.
*Industry:* change of industry, say chemicals industry to academia.
*Function:* change of job function.

Normally, you would only look to change one of these dimensions at any one time. How many of us look seriously at more than one of these options at a time? Probably only a few of us.

Many opportunities lie outside our usual line of sight in other industries, companies, countries, cultures and job functions. In an ideal world we want to look at all of these opportunities and not just the obvious ones that present themselves. It could simply be the opportunity to learn a new foreign language.

### Case study from Bill's career

I was working in London as the Group Advertising Sales Manager for a successful weekly teenage magazine. I received an offer from a French publishing company Bayard Presse as a Rights Manager based in their international head office in Paris. The role was substantially different from anything I had previously encountered in my career. It was a horizontal move. Part of my rationale for taking this position was my dream of becoming a fluent French speaker. I changed all aspects of my business and social life.

*Culture:* both business and social.
*Location:* London to Paris.
*Language:* English to French.
*Industry:* Advertising sales to book publishing.
*Function:* Sales to international publishing rights.

How did I manage the transition from being a salesman to becoming a buyer of international publishing rights? Many of the behaviours that made me a successful advertising salesman in the first place could be transferred to my new role. I was an effective communicator as I was continually trying to perfect my written and oral presentation style. I had the ability to negotiate whilst fully understanding all the ramifications of the process and how it might affect the overall outcome. I was commercially astute. However, there were two differences: I was conducting business in French and buying instead of selling.

# Dangers of CV Thinking

One of the current dangers in changing function or industry is that many employers, recruiters and executive search companies use 'CV Thinking'. For the 'CV Thinker' new opportunities are constrained and defined by the last position you held. Great opportunities are missed and companies miss out on suitable candidates. Sometimes, the only candidates a company sees are the closest matches to the category experience. This is a shame, as there are many candidates who could provide additional value and stretch by delivering a strong, broad range of skills and experience that would be suitable not only for the role today but also for where organizations want to go in the future. This 'CV Thinking' can lead to missed opportunities for you and the potential employer. We could all benefit from being more open with our requirements.

## Case study from Bill's career

I suffered from 'CV Thinking' on my return to the UK from Australia. I thought like a CV. The recruitment agencies whom I had asked to help me were also 'CV Thinkers'. I prepared my new and gleaming CV concentrating on the role I had just completed. I wrote good solid facts highlighting my achievements.

Through 'CV Thinking', I had branded and positioned myself as a new media agency director, nothing else. I could not understand why the job I had held in Australia suddenly seemed to be the only thing I had ever done. All my work prior to this was deemed irrelevant. What had happened to the previous ten years of my working life? Had they slipped through a time warp? I was sure I had put everything in my CV and even checked this numerous times. About halfway through the recruitment process, I began thinking differently. What could I offer other companies? What did they find interesting in me? I had begun my initial 'EP Thinking'. There was a resounding clash as my 'EP Thinking' met my 'CV Thinking'.

I spent many hours on the phone and in meetings with recruitment agencies explaining I was interested in not only the new-media agency roles but also wider-ranging positions. It was my persistence on this occasion that won the day. I had just not realized the recruitment industry were doing exactly what I had asked of them. The problem did not lie with them. It lay firmly at my feet. Or to be more accurate, it was the fault of a good CV not being able to do the job I had asked of it.

I secured a senior marketing position in the world of financial services. The financial services industry was a place that was unfamiliar and where I had no direct experience. What I had was a set of Transferable Assets that meant I could add real value to the company and look at the issues faced with a fresh outlook. Importantly, I was not going to regurgitate something I had done in a previous financial services company. It allowed me to produce unique innovative and creative work. It showed me how cross-pollination of ideas from one industry sector to another could add real value to the bottom line.

When I came to leaving the financial services company, I was faced by the very same problem as before: 'CV Thinking' in an EP world.

But, again I transferred from one industry sector to another, as I had understood that the employers were interested in who I am, how I do it, and what I do.

**"Good people are flexible, never stop learning and applying and generally don't just stay in one category industry; they also are not threatened by change and evolution, they thrive on it."**

Mark Bailey, Board Director of Leo Burnett Advertising: Australia

# Coping with redundancy

No one plans for redundancy. Unfortunately, it just happens. Redundancy is often associated with a downturn of not only a company but also an industry sector. If this is the case, trying to get straight back into that particular market sector could be a long process. There will be a large number of equally qualified individuals vying for an ever-decreasing number of positions. It is therefore a good idea to study your Transferable Assets and consider options in other functions and other potentially more lucrative industries. This ultimately reflects the changing work patterns. Many people put all their effort into their current role and rely on the organization to deliver their career. Redundancy may be your reward when the employer faces marked changes. You need to be continually adapting and learning, gaining experiences and broadening your base.

**"Learning new skills is an ongoing process and needs to be positively pursued at all times by everyone whatever position they are in. When you are made redundant it is too late."**

Iain Herbertson, CEO of Manpower UK

## The demands of interim management

Interim management is becoming a lifestyle choice for many senior executives. As a profession, it has also been responding to changes in the work environment. Several years ago, interim management was

# Learning new ongoing process positively

concerned with covering maternity leave and not rocking the boat. In today's uncertain world, interim management is concerned more with delivering and speeding up the way companies run. They come to troubleshoot a project or manage a business function. They need to have specific market knowledge but also a broad commercial base. They hit the decks running, identifying the key issues, developing action plans, bringing teams with them, running the implementation, smashing through obstacles and bringing a sense of urgency. Interim managers need to display a sense of the key competencies that can match their specific market knowledge to the wider imperative to deliver change. Interim managers have unwittingly been using EP Thinking, but they have not had the vehicle to use it in. This has changed with the arrival of the Elevator Pitch.

## Experience is diverse

You may be returning to work after an absence of a couple of years for whatever reason. It could have been to raise a family, to study Inca art in South America, or to circumnavigate the globe in a yacht. You will have gained valuable experience that is not always that easy to capture, e.g. the teamwork and leadership skills that are necessary to sail around the world. This experience helps build your Career DNA.

# skills is an and needs to be pursued

## Work experience versus Transferable Assets

Think back to how you sold yourself at your first-ever job interview after university or college. You related behaviours and shared experiences about college life and made them connect to your new working life. Essentially, you had identified your Transferable Assets. Some of us may have started our new careers and then, a couple of years down the line, decided we should take a new direction. You were then caught in a catch-22 position. The roles required experience. Why is it that two years earlier you could use your Transferable Assets to land a job, whereas now your worth is measured by work experience? The Elevator Pitch redefines your relationship to work experience and allows you to start again.

## Better and more successful interviews

The Elevator Pitch is your initial marketing tool. Like all marketing initiatives, the message needs to be put to the right target market and contain relevant content to fulfil the target markets needs.

The interview is a business meeting. Your aim is to put your point of view across to sell an idea, concept or proposition, communicate a message, or sell yourself in a style that is completely irresistible and worth remembering. They can't help but want to buy you.

# The Elevator Pitch

Traditionally the CV has been the document used to control the pace and direction of the interview. As mentioned previously the CV concentrates on your historical events and spreads its net very wide to include information that is not relevant and needs to be deciphered. It does not focus on the information pertinent and relevant to the vacancy.

Using your Elevator Pitch to set the agenda for an interview bolsters the proceedings because it is clear, concise and focused. Its focus is on those parts of your career that you know to be relevant for the role. The inclusion of only relevant content saves precious time, increasing the likelihood of the interview addressing only the salient points.

The interview is a two-way street. It requires direction and a fine balance of control from the interviewee. Too many times it is the interviewer doing all the driving.

The Elevator Pitch is the road map to guide you through a successful meeting and help attain the desired results.

You can use the Elevator Pitch to control the flow of information. Good negotiation rests on what you say, how you say it and when you say it. The CV contains your whole life story. The Elevator Pitch contains only pertinent information. You can emphasize different aspects of your career through tailored Elevator Pitches. They are easy to amend to create bespoke packages. This is especially important the deeper one goes through the recruitment process. At each step, you learn more about the competencies that define success for this position

# is your initial
# marketing tool

# You will **never**

and organization. Your Elevator Pitch can become more refined. The decision on what to highlight and when to highlight is down to you. This is only possible with an Elevator Pitch.

Jack Gratton, CEO of Major Players, the UK's leading recruitment agency for the marketing services industry, produced an Elevator Pitch for the book. In his own words, this would '… definitely get me in front of people, but I would probably take another to the meeting to set the inteview agenda.' By careful use of the Elevator Pitch one can gain control of meetings. The Elevator Pitch is about the quality and relevance of information. This creates the first vital impressions.

Your Elevator Pitch is physical evidence of the synergy between your competencies and the vacancy on offer. It is the best document to leave behind.

One of the true benefits of the Elevator Pitch is its ability to make sure you stand out from the crowd and you are put into the 'Yes' pile, as 'No' and 'Maybe' are not good enough. You have gained the competitive advantage.

## Help your referee

The job of your referee is to help secure your new job, by giving further evidence of who you are, how you do it, and what you do. They add real value. You need them to speak eloquently about you from their position of authority and about your Transferable Assets. The Elevator Pitch ensures your referee can see which direction you are taking and which Transferable Assets you are using. Anticipate some of the

# **need** a CV again

questions that could be asked of your referee and brief them accordingly. Give them all the help and direction you can.

## Highlighting and uniting your career

As the world changes and traditional career paths fracture your Elevator Pitch unites and highlights your career choices (Figure 4.2).

Why will the Elevator Pitch take over from where the CV left off? Put simply, it is better. If we compare them head to head by dissecting their respective strengths, weaknesses, opportunities and threats, you will easily see the differences (Figures 4.3 and 4.4).

You will never need a CV again.

The Elevator Pitch is a buyer-pull view of the world. It talks a universally recognized language and emphasizes fit. It unites variety and highlights singularity of career. It provides the answer to how you do things. It reduces extraneous information to the core. It places you in control of your life and allows you to release information at key points in the negotiating process.

The Elevator Pitch is the 21st Century successor to the CV.

| Career | CV | EP |
|---|---|---|
| Industry variety | Dissipates | Unites |
| Functional variety | Dissipates | Unites |
| Singular industry | Not differentiating | Highlights |
| Singular function | Not differentiating | Highlights |

**Figure 4.2**   Highlighting and uniting your career

| Strengths | Weaknesses |
|---|---|
| Historical, rational<br>Conventional and traditional – safe<br>Universal<br>Shows why you were paid for previous years<br>Chronological – shows consistency<br>Linear | Cannot easily answer 'What does this person do or offer me? What is their value add?'<br>Contains all information rather than pertinent, relevant and selective information in a 'Take it or leave it menu'<br>Hides your value beneath chronological façade<br>Fails to emphasize fit between you and the job<br>Need for someone else to decipher and understand your real value<br>Exacerbates flaws in the interview process<br>Used to create barriers to entry not opportunity<br>People get them wrong<br>Seller push world view: fails to emphasize fit between you and the job. Not distinguishing and distinctive – lacks soul<br>Static, linear, rational, historical & conventional<br>Common language with uncommon tongue |
| Opportunities | Threats |
| Opportunity to answer 'What does this person do or offer me? What is their value add?'<br>Improved way to provide relevant, pertinent and selective information<br>Better sales document<br>Increase flexibility<br>To showcase your future value | The Elevator Pitch |

**Figure 4.3**   The weakness of your CV

| Strengths | Weaknesses |
|---|---|
| Easily answers 'What does this person do or offer me? What is their value add?' Pertinent, relevant and selective information in a 'bespoke menu'. Reduces extraneous information to relevant data Showcases your real value Emphasizes fit between you and the job – buyer pull view of the world No need for someone else to decipher and understand your real value. Establishes common language – no code, no deciphering required Maximizes opportunity in hiring Easy to get right and not make basic mistakes Dynamic, non-linear, modern Unites career variety and highlights career singularity Proven ability to deliver, forward looking, establishes rapport, flexibility and adaptability Results driven Aids recruitment – saves recruiter time and effort by highlighting relevant information in a concise format You gain greater control of selection process from primary contact to interview | Not yet accepted as the new currency |
| Opportunities | Threats |
| To become the new currency of recruitment | Closed minds |

**Figure 4.4**  The benefits of your Elevator Pitch

# 5

# Top-floor Elevator Pitches

We would like to welcome all of you who thought this was the first page of the book. We know this is an obvious mistake that anyone of us could make!

We would recommend a look at the rest of the book as it is really quite good. After all you have bought a copy. It seems a shame not to make the most of it.

In this chapter we have pulled together a collection of Elevator Pitches from real people from many walks of life. They range from pilots to office managers, from entrepreneurs to advertising people, from mechanical engineers to veterinary nurses, from publishers to politicians. They demonstrate the flexibility and universal approach of the Elevator Pitch and the people who use it.

Both Mara Goldstein, a senior member of the British Civil Service, and John Baldwin, a senior mechanical engineer, have been good enough to allow us to publish not only their Elevator Pitches but also their traditional CVs. We have included these so direct comparison between the two can be made.

# Elevator Pitches to be hard-hitting, no-nonsense

John's CV is relatively unorthodox as it is too long. It also fails because it does not prioritize pertinent and relevant information. His traditional CV has focused on what his roles were, not what he achieved or how he achieved them. Quite simply, it does not tell the reader who John is and what he does. Although John's Elevator Pitch is shorter than his CV, it manages to convey John's capabilities and personality. John's Elevator Pitch is pertinent, relevant, and makes the right impression.

Mara is a high achiever. She has fast-tracked through the ranks of the Civil Service in the UK and the European Commission. Mara's CV contains much information but it is a list of committees, functions and responsibilities. It is hard to understand why Mara has been successful. Her CV fails on the key criteria of readability, relevance and impression. On the other hand, her Elevator Pitch, which is based on a set of required Civil Service Competencies, is more resonant than her CV and is a succinct and powerful document that captures the Mara her friends know. Mara has crammed much into her life and her Elevator Pitch reflects this. She clearly feels the Elevator Pitch gets to the heart of what she actually does and who she really is.

# are designed no-fuss, strategic personal sales documents

You will see many examples of Elevator Pitches. They are designed to be hard-hitting, no-fuss, no-nonsense strategic personal sales documents.

You will also see a job description for a veterinary sales manager. We then give the job candidate's analysis broken down into its component Transferable Assets and the Elevator Pitch she wrote to secure the position.

Ken Livingstone, the first elected Mayor of London has been kind enough to write his Elevator Pitch for the book.

We would like to thank our friends and colleagues, for all their help in this chapter.

Most of the following Elevator Pitches can be printed on one side of A4 paper. Some of the Elevator Pitches reproduced in the book will by necessity fall on 3 pages, due to the size of the book.

Here's a list of the CVs and Elevator pitches that follow.

➡ John Baldwin's EP

➡ John Baldwin's CV

➡ Mara Goldstein's EP

➡ Mara Goldstein's CV

➡ Nancy Prendegast's EP

➡ Bill Faust's EP

➡ Michael Faust's EP

➡ Marc Schavemaker's EP

➡ Mark Bailey's EP

➡ Louise Medley's EP

➡ Ken Livingstone's EP

- Darren Fell's EP

- Justine Cobb's EP

- Jack Gratton's EP

- Richard Davies' EP

- Charlie Dobres' EP

- Job brief and answers by Laura Neilson's EP

## JOHN BALDWIN | SENIOR MECHNICAL ENGINEER

**2 Doughton Road, Gloucestershire GL21 6PW, UK**
**Mobile: 44(0) xxxx xxxx, Home: 44(0) 1555 xxx xxx, E-mail: John@anywhere.com**

Customer-focused, intelligent risk taker. Direction setter of inventive solutions with the willingness to absorb situations and get on with it.

28 years' leadership of $multimillion mechanical engineering projects in the international oil industry.

| | |
|---|---|
| **Analytical communication** | My engineering background gives me an analytical nature and, as GM and VP, I chaired weekly production meetings and successfully analyzed critical path processes to keep delivery schedules on track through the disruptive period of a plant-expansion programme. |
| | Participation in major tender authorship together with personal presentations to key account clients dramatically improved bid package content and contributed to four new account and territory successes in a 2-year period while maintaining all existing accounts. |
| **Hands on outside the box** | 8 years in field service management in international offshore and onshore operations have given me a sound hands-on industry competency. |
| | At GM Kvaerner Oilfield Products – Middle East, I instigated and set up a unique JV manufacturing partnership in Iran, resulting in a market entry over a 4-year period generating sales revenue of $5m. This continues to develop and grow. This was very much an 'outside the box' strategy not initially considered workable by some. |
| **Supportive and approachable management style** | I managed 12 expatriate employees in 3 Middle-Eastern countries, most of whom were family accompanied. I had responsibility for the equitable administration of company policy in areas such as housing, local benefits, schooling, vehicles, home leaves, etc., requiring a fair and reasonable approach with even-handed treatment for all. Living conditions in the late 1970s were trying and required a supportive and approachable management style. |

| **Lateral move flexibility** | Accepted a lateral move as a career-development opportunity and a chance to develop from scratch a complete sales and marketing presence where none had existed. This resulted in sales exceeding $5m/annum within 2 years, and a threefold increase in head count plus an additional district office set-up. |
| --- | --- |
| | I am a well-rounded individual having demonstrated a flexibility that has progressed me through 10 senior positions in 10 postings (6 international) with 3 multinational companies that have required a solid mix of business and pleasure with colleagues and clients. Throughout, a supportive wife and family have ably encouraged me. |
| **Career history** | **Kvaerner Oilfield Products    1996 to present**<br>Regional Sales Manager, Europe, Africa and Middle East – based Head Office London<br>General Manager, Middle East – based Dubai<br>General Manager and Vice President, Asia Pacific – based Singapore<br><br>**FMC Corporation UK Ltd    1979–1995**<br>Area Sales Manager, Europe and North Africa<br>Key Account Manager – based London<br>Regional Sales Manager, Europe, Africa and Middle East – based France<br>Key Account Manager, based London<br>Regional Sales Manager, Australasia – based Melbourne<br><br>**McEvoy Oilfield Equipment Ltd    1973–1979**<br>Senior Sales Engineer – based Singapore<br>Sales and Service Manager – based Scotland<br><br>**Peglar Hattersley and Newman Hender Ltd    1966–1973**<br><br>**Languages:** Fluent business French |

## CV JOHN BALDWIN

| | |
|---|---|
| **Full name:** | John Baldwin |
| **Date of birth:** | 21 October 19xx |
| **Nationality:** | British |
| **Status:** | Married, daughter 31 years, son 27 years |
| **UK address:** | 2 Doughton Road |
| | Gloucestershire |
| | GL21 6PW |
| **UK tel:** | +44 (0)1666 xxx xxx |
| **Office tel:** | +44 1666 xxx xxx |
| **Mobile tel:** | +44 xxxxx xxx xxx |
| **Email:** | email@anywhere.com |

**Education record**

Sir William Romney's Grammar School, Tetbury

Mid-Gloucestershire College of Technology

**Qualifications**

Higher National Certificate in Mechanical Engineering

**Memberships**

Society of Petroleum Engineers

**Proficiencies**

Microsoft Office Suite™

**Languages**

Conversational French

**Courses and training completed**

Managing Interpersonal Relationships

The Crosby Quality Course

Effective Financial Management

Proposal Planning

Managing Performance through Effective Leadership

**Employment record**

**April 2001–present**

**Regional Sales Manager, Europe, Africa and Middle East (KOP Surface Equipment) – based Head Office London, reporting to the International Sales Manager and VP in Houston**

The company refocus on surface product technology in response to a decline in major subsea project work worldwide has resulted in an expansion in territory and customer base where surface and onshore development is expanding. The establishment of sales structures for continued growth in the Middle East and Iran, including the establishment of an Iranian JV manufacturing entity and a coverage of North African potential, have been key areas of activity to date.

Recognition of further opportunities in the European, North Sea and Eastern Europe areas, together with the concentration of major international operating companies in London, Paris, The Hague and Milan, has made European sales coverage of prime importance, and increased tender participation through a London presence is evident.

**1998–April 2001**

**General Manager, Kvaerner Oilfield Products (KOP) Middle East – based Dubai, reporting to the president in Singapore**

Following a 2-year period as VP in Singapore, and despite a successful trading year, the sudden and catastrophic Asian economic crises coupled with a record low oil price, made sweeping economies in the

John Baldwin's CV continued

Far East operation essential as a matter of good business practice. New markets and new accounts were required to maintain the business and, as VP marketing, I had already identified the Middle East as a growth area for KOP.

I transferred to Dubai in September of 1998 to start up KOP's first Middle-Eastern venture, with the establishment of a representative office in Dubai in support of existing business and in pursuit of new business development in the area. To date, this has resulted in exploration equipment business with Total for Iranian projects, and the company's qualification with PDO, Oman, NIOC – Iran and Occidental in Qatar. Other major accounts are in process, and the company is on target to secure a first-year budgeted order intake for the Middle East of over $2m. As of this date, the Middle East now accounts for 75% of all new quotations activity for the region.

**1996–1998**

**General Manager and Vice President, Kvaerner Oilfield Products, Asia Pacific – based Singapore, reporting to the President**

I initially joined KOP as Marketing Manager and was promoted to GM and VP. The company closed its Singapore manufacturing operation to expand a new facility in Batam Island, Indonesia. I was heavily involved with the start-up operations at Batam, while maintaining normal business activity through the start-up period.

KOP maintained a staff of 25 people in Singapore with 160 people at the Batam plant. In addition to general management duties, I was also responsible for sales and marketing, with the internal quotations department reporting to me. Despite the considerable traumas of the plant relocation, KOP experienced its best-ever order intake for the region in 1998, exceeding $25m for the first time and establishing four major new accounts and three new territory market entries.

Regional Managers in Thailand, India and Australia reported to me for sales-related matters, and I chaired the weekly production meetings at the Batam plant. Since the president was responsible for all KOP product lines, he maintained an extremely busy travel schedule, thus leaving me to run all routine administration in the region for both manufacturing and marketing. Performance-related bonuses were paid in both years.

### 1995–1996

**Area Sales Manager, Europe and North Africa, and Key Account Manager FMC Corporation UK Ltd, Petroleum Equipment and Systems Division**

Based in London and reporting to the international marketing director at the manufacturing plant in Dunfermline, Scotland. Supervising a sales team of 5 company sales engineers and 5 international sales and stockists agencies.

The role included an additional responsibility for 2 key accounts (BP and Philips Petroleum), which were managed personally. International and domestic business travel accounted for 60% of time, putting me in contact with the company's manufacturing plants in both the UK and France. Preparation of account plans, inbound budgets and operating budgets was my responsibility for the area.

Sales for the area in 1994 were $15m, and 1995 exceeded $18m. Products marketed included production and exploration wellhead equipment, subsea drilling and production systems, drilling tools, and high-pressure control valves.

▶

John Baldwin's CV continued

This role required a regular interface with engineering and commercial contract managers, particularly in the preparation phase of high-value quotations and subsequent clarification and negotiation meetings with clients. The key account role developed close interpersonal relationships with clients and created the basis for preferred supplier status before tender release, so leading to the stronger position of incumbent on future tenders.

Personnel administration included the setting of objectives and performance criteria and subsequent performance reviews. Agents and distributors were visited regularly and, when necessary, agreements were modified or terminated. The appointment of reliable agents was a crucial part of the job, and FMC enjoyed a reputation for long-term agency relationships for which I am happy to take some credit.

The position relocated from France in November 1994 when product line sourcing was largely relocated to the UK plant, making the logistics of territory management and interface with both plants more convenient from the London base.

**1991–1995**

**Regional Sales Manager, Europe, Africa and Middle East, FMC Europe SA-Equipment Petrolier**

Reporting to the International Marketing Manager then located in Brussels. Resident in Sens, France, working from the manufacturing plant. This role was largely similar to that described above, but with the additional responsibility of West Africa and part of the Middle East (Oman and Qatar).

The number of subordinates was between 8 and 10 company Sales Engineers and up to 8 agencies, with annual sales growing to $30m for material sourced from the French plant in1994.

At this time, Oman and Qatar were a part of our sales territory for historical sourcing reasons, and I was instrumental in completing a market survey and instigating initial discussions with our agent in Oman (who I had appointed in 1979) with a view to setting up a joint venture manufacturing plant in Muscat. This plant is now operational and has secured 75% of a $12m market for FMC in Oman with potential for exports to other GCC states in the Gulf.

During this period, I was resident with my wife in Sens, France and by necessity became familiar with the language and culture. The final year of my posting in France also included responsibility for internal sales management (quotations) and a small field service team of 5 engineers.

**1988–1991**

**Key Account Manager, FMC Corporation UK Ltd – based London, reporting to the Regional Marketing Manager in Dunfermline**

Key accounts included BP, Shell and British Gas. Inbound in 1991 for these accounts exceeded $8m and included production wellhead equipment for the BP Bruce platform in the UK North Sea, Shell Tern, and British Gas Morcambe Bay.

**1983–1988**

**Regional Sales Manager, Australasia – based Melbourne, Victoria for FMC Australia Ltd, reporting to the Marketing Manager in Singapore**

**John Baldwin's CV continued**

Small sales and service team of three people covering a relatively small market, but very large geographically. The territory included New Zealand and Papua New Guinea. Business was supported primarily by local stocking and warehousing operations in Melbourne and Perth, and focused on the low-tech end of a niche market, which enabled us to compete with a locally based manufacturer of petroleum equipment.

The logistics involved in importing from the Singapore plant and distributing and servicing a vast territory were a considerable challenge and enabled me to develop a good understanding of the distribution side of the business.

### 1979–1983

**Area Manager, Middle East – based Dubai, UAE and reporting to the International Marketing Manager in Houston Texas**

Territory included all Gulf states, Pakistan and Turkey. I was responsible for a sales and service operation extending to a total of 12 expatriates based in Dubai, Abu Dhabi and Muscat. At this time, FMC business in the Middle East was in its infancy, and the appointment of agents in Bahrain, Kuwait and Oman were key objectives.

The Oman agency has since developed into a JV manufacturing agreement, and all other representative agreements initiated by me are still effective. Travel requirements were extensive and sometimes arduous, while 24hr service commitments were demanding.

The early 1980s were boom days in the petroleum industry, and sales figures can be misleading, but sales exceeded $20m in all years, even though some personnel rationalization to reduce expatriate costs became necessary by 1982. I consider this to have been an excellent character- and experience-building post.

### 1976–1979

**Senior Sales Engineer, McEvoy Oilfield Equipment Ltd (then owned by Rockwell Corp.) – based Singapore, reporting to the Sales Manager in Singapore**

Sales and service of petroleum production equipment throughout the Far East, India and Pakistan. This was my first expatriate assignment in a pure sales role but also with some field service back-up responsibility in support of other company bases in Malaysia and Brunei.

### 1973–1978

**Sales and Service Manager, McEvoy Oilfield Equipment Ltd, based Aberdeen, Scotland, reporting to the UK Sales Manager in London**

Supervision of 3 sales and service engineers covering the company's business in the UK and Norwegian sectors of the North Sea. Management of a service depot and basic repair and rework shop.

### 1966–1973

**Peglar Hattersley and Newman Hender Ltd UK**

Completed a college engineering course and moved to various production and design positions in the valve-manufacturing departments of these companies. Finished in the design drawing office and later the service departments engaged in international field service work.

## DR MARA GOLDSTEIN PRIVATE SECRETARY TO THE HOME SECRETARY

55 Orchard Road, London, UK
Tel.: 44 (0) 20 xxxx xxxx, E-mail: marag@somewhere.com

I like to think that dynamic change happens in places I work. I only do jobs I enjoy so I tend to be good at them.

I make a difference through strategic guidance which empowers change, through creativity and by motivating my team.

I have spent 10 years in the Civil Service after gaining my doctorate in law.

| Achieving results of high quality and value | Analyzing information, planning strategy, managing change and delivering. |
| --- | --- |
| | As Private Secretary to the Home Secretary fast analysis of a wide range of issues was required. I had some direct input into strategic work, for example, during the problems in 1999 at the UK Passport Office, when I worked with senior management, and I had daily involvement in the Pinochet extradition case. |
| | In the European Commission, I developed its strategy on international police co-operation including Europol and designed and delivered its strategy on Trafficking in Women, often working opposite more senior colleagues from national administrations. |
| | In the Home Office International Unit I planned the 1998 UK Presidency of the EU. |
| | I manage personal change proactively through regular job and organization changes. I have always encouraged organizational change in my working environment: by setting up a unit in the European Commission; by close involvement in the management of the Home Office International unit, including having the main responsibility for staffing and organization. |
| | I am keen to encourage improved business processes through more effective use of new technologies. |
| | As Private Secretary, I was responsible for the daily delivery of the Home Secretary's needs across a wide range of subjects. |
| Leadership and personal responsibility | Leading team, motivating and showing good judgement. |
| | Recruited staff whilst acting head of the police co-operation unit of the European Commission. |
| | I set up the Presidency team during the UK Presidency, and kept 5 staff motivated and largely in good humour, whilst working at high pressure, for over a year, delivering a complex organisational requirement for the Department. |

I held short seminars for other unit staff to involve them in the Presidency and ran Department wide seminars and language training to encourage wider involvement.

As Private Secretary, I developed a working relationship with much of the Department, trying to motivate staff who were often working under pressure, to get delivery of the Home Secretary's requirements.

I also had direct involvement in high profile issues, such as the Afghan hijack, by helping to develop and implement strategy.

Responsibility for the delivery of the Home Secretary's work required constant rapid adjustments, as in previous roles.

**Being open and communicating well**

Writing and speaking effectively and being able to persuade and influence others.

I have much experience of speaking in public and presenting arguments as Commission Representative in Council work groups. I made speeches on JHA matters for senior officials from Accession States.

I wrote the Commission's Communication on Trafficking in Women and was responsible for briefing senior officials, Commissioners and MEPs on a range of police and other issues, both in writing and orally.

I'd d regular submissions for UK ministers as Presidency Co-ordinator.

I had extensive experience in minute writing as secretary to working group on Europol (minutes for all member states), minute writer for the Commission for five working groups, and then minuting Home Secretary meetings.

I communicated the Home Secretary's views and requests to the department in writing and orally, and attempted to persuade officials to do/not to do things.

**Valuing the people we work with and their diversity**

Especially promoting equal opportunity, delegating effectively and developing staff.

I recruited and trained staff in the Commission and the Home Office. I have worked with mainly female staff, but have always sought the best person for the job.

I recruited and trained 40 Presidency volunteers, giving development and experience to Home Office staff in a wide variety of jobs. That group had high ethnic minority representation. After attending Race Equality Workshops, I offered to provide shadowing experience for ethnic minority staff interested in working in a Minister's Office and became an associate member of the Home Office Network.

Whilst in the International Unit, I secured a new training budget and ensured all my staff attended appropriate developmental training every year, including at least one day of external training, in addition to organization of language training both in the unit and Home Office.

I trained and motivated unit staff through seminars and projects and have always delegated effectively when staff available.

| | |
|---|---|
| **Managing resources** | Getting the best from available resources and balancing resources and demands. |
| | I keep all available resources of all types under constant review. |
| | Financial Resources: during the Presidency, I had day to day responsibility for the Home Office entire budget (reporting to Head of Unit). I negotiated with outside suppliers and local authorities and saved some £150,000 on predicted expenditure of £500,000. |
| | I encourage thrift in the office by use of standard class travel where appropriate, and set up internal recycling schemes which saved natural resources and money. A Home Office paper saving initiative came out at a monthly saving of 12 reams. This motivated other staff, who organized internal glass and plastic recycling. |
| | I have always had to make decisions about priorities. |
| **Working in partnership with others** | Especially developing good working relationships and managing conflict. |
| | I was known as an effective operator in the European Commission, where much depends on contact and communication. I encouraged colleagues to share information and work to common goals, and built a wide network of colleagues around the EU. |
| | I think I had generally good working relationships during the Presidency. |
| | I developed ways of retaining relaxed relationships under pressure in Private Office. |

**Career history**

**Foreign & Commonwealth Office:**   **2001–present**
Deputy Head of European Union Department (internal)

**Home Office**   **1998–2001**
Private Secretary to the Home Secretary

**Home Office**   **1997–1998**
Presidency Co-ordinator 1998 UK Presidency of the EU

**European Commission**   **1994–1997**
Secondment to the Task Force on Justice and Home Affairs, Detached National Expert

**Cabinet Office, Secondment to Home Office**   **1992–1994**
Higher Executive Officer (Development – Europe)

**University Of Passau**   **1988–1992**
Assistant in Law Faculty

**Languages**
Native English, bilingual German and moderate French.

**Music**
I am a member of the Academy of St. Martin in the Fields Chorus, Tallis Chamber Choir, New London Chamber Choir and Joyful Company of Singers. I founded and sang in a h ghly successful madrigal choir in Passau.

**Other**
I have received 4 awards and scholarships.

## CV MARA GOLDSTEIN

**DOB/POB**     10 March 19xx, Sheffield England

**Experience**

**Since 9/2001 Foreign and Commonwealth Office, London SW1P**

**Deputy Head of European Union Department (Internal)**

Overseeing departmental dossiers, briefs and submissions. Giving strategic direction to team and priorities in the department.

**10/1998–7/2001 Home Office, London SW1**

**Private Secretary to the Home Secretary**

Particular responsibility for European and International Affairs, Immigration and Asylum, Judicial Co-operation including Extradition, Family Policy.

**7/1998–9/1998 Bundesministerium des Inneres, Austria**

**Secondment**

Assisted with Presidency work on the 1998 Austria Presidency of the EU.

**3/1997–6/1998 Home Office, London SW1**

**Presidency Co-ordinator for 1998 UK presidency of the EU**

I was in charge of a section of 6 people with responsibility for the logistical aspects of the Presidency, co-ordination of policy internally and with other Government Departments, and liaison with the Council Secretariat, UK Representation in Brussels, European Commission and European Parliament. Responsibilities included advice to Ministers on aspects of the Presidency, co-ordination of the calendar of Brussels meetings, organization of UK based meetings and training for Home Office staff. I also oversaw inward and outward international Ministerial visits.

### 2/1994–1 /1997 European Commission, Brussels

**Secondment to the Task Force on Justice and Home Affairs, Detached National Expert**

I helped establish the unit on Police Co-operation and represented the Commission in Council Working Groups on Europol, Police Co-operation, and Drugs and Organized Crime. Responsibilities included preparation of Council meetings, liaison with Interpol, support to Commissioners at European Parliament hearings, and lecturing on the Third Pillar.

### 9/1992–2/1994 Cabinet Office, London

**Higher Executive Officer (Development – Europe)**

Secondment to the Home Office. I was posted in the European Police Secretariat, where I had an overview of TREVI Working Groups II and III. I was secretary to the Ad Hoc Working Group on EUROPOL, and was involved in the work on the draft Convention to establish EUROPOL.

### 9/1988–9/1992 University of Passau

**Assistant in the Law Faculty/ Part-time lectureship**

Teaching British constitutional law and the English legal system, with additional courses in British politics. In 1990, I was offered a permanent full-time lectureship in English law (to administer and teach external LLB students), which I turned down in order to complete my doctoral thesis.

**8/1989:** Hague Academy of International Law – Summer Session on the Law of Asylum.

**Summer 1998:** Research assistant to Dr R. O. Plender QC, revising new edition of Plender and Usher's *Cases and Materials on the Law of the European Communities*.

**1989–1990 and 3/1992:** Teaching beginners' courses in English language.

**1–7/1987:** Private tuition in English language for 'Abitur' (A-level) candidates.

**1981–1987:** Various summer and part-time jobs, including practical training with Boodle Hatfield Solicitors and much legal secretarial work.

**Education**

**7/1992 University of Passau, Germany**
Dr Juris – thesis on European Community Competence in the Law of Asylum ('Die Kompetenzen der Europaischen Gemeinschaften zur Regelung des Asylrechts').

**1984–1988 King's College, London**

**7/1988** LLB, Dip. Ger. Law, AKC.

**1986–7 Passau University, FRG, Germany**
Diploma in German Law, awarded with 12.8 points out of 18, the average being around 5.5.

**1981–83 King's School, Worcester**

GCE A-Levels in German (A), English (B), Music (C).

GCE S-Level in German (Merit).

**1970–1981 Sheffield High School for Girls**

**1981–1982** 4 GCE O-Levels (A), 6 GCE O-Levels (B).

**Awards**

**2/1997**

1-month study visit of the USA at the invitation of the USA Overseas Visitor's Programme. Participation in the Young European Leaders project.

**7/1993**

1500-ECU publication grant for doctoral thesis from the Commission of the European Communities.

**1986–1987**

Scholarship from the British Chamber of Commerce in Germany to aid legal studies in Germany.

**1986–1987**

Scholarship from the Erasmus programme of the European Communities to aid legal studies in Germany.

**Languages** Native English, bilingual German, moderate French.

## Additional qualifications/skills

**5/1982** Full Driving Licence.

**4/1984** Secretarial Diploma from Sight and Sound College including Typing at 60 wpm, Shorthand at 80 wpm and Word Processing.

## Further achievements and interests

**8/1994** Participant in 'Young Konigswinter' Anglo-German Forum.

**7/1993** Participation in the Wilton Park Young Anglo-German Forum, administered by the Foreign and Commonwealth Office.

**1990–1991** Committee membership of the 'Studenten fur Passau', a non-aligned political party in the local elections.

**1989–1990** Secretary of the 'Passauer Studentendorf e.V'.

**1987–1988** Secretary of the King's College/Passau Society.

**1984–1985** Participation in the King's College 'Borstal Project'.

## Music

I am a member of the Academy of St. Martin in the Fields Chorus, Tallis Chamber Choir, New London Chamber Choir and Joyful Company of Singers. Whilst in Passau I founded and sang in a highly successful madrigal choir. As a student, I was on the committee for the University of London Music Society and librarian for the University of London Choir and at school I organized the 6th form music society. I have been a member of many choirs, including the National Youth Choir, and used to be principal oboe player for the Midland Youth Orchestra and

Worcester Cathedral Chamber Orchestra. I have qualifications in Associated Board Grade VIII Distinction Oboe, Grade VI Singing and Grade V Piano.

**Sport**

**1981** Captain of the tennis team at Sheffield High School.

## NANCY M. PRENDERGAST | BUSINESS COMMUNICATOR

**The Mews House, London, UK**
**Tel: 44 (0) 20 xxxx xxxx, E-mail: nmprender@yahoo.co.uk**

I am a strategic business communicator with a proven ability to exploit commercial opportunities. A respected people manager and team player, I have guided teams of up to 20 consultants to excel. With a broad understanding of the marketing mix and of new media channels, I apply classic principles to new ways of doing business. I am a creative and innovative problem solver who gets results.

My experience ranges from positioning and launching software products for blue-chip companies to helping build the brands and media profiles of many innovative new businesses to running one of the UK's most talked about PR companies. My fascination with evolving media channels, grasp of technology and its implications on how we work and live, and cross-cultural interests fuel my career ambitions.

**Focuses on the commercial**

Played key role in building team, client portfolio and revenues of young PR agency, helping to exploit high-growth web and mobile commerce market opportunities. Directly responsible for revenues in 2000 of more than £850K – nearly half the agency total. An aggressive growth strategy culminated in Gnash Communications being named the UK's fastest growing PR consultancy, April 2001.

**Thinks strategically**

Identified a gap in the market for PR services to support start-up companies, devised a set of new products to extend Gnash's offering. These include pan-European best-practice agency network; position workshop; communications plan boot camp; agency search and selection; and viral PR programme. These services added more than £3/4m to agency revenues over 18 months.

**Solves problems**

Reflecting a VC client's conservative approach to media, created work-around programmes to meet PR objectives. A portfolio outreach programme significantly raised the profile of the client's investments and thereby the client's own profile. Programme was subsequently used as a model by client's agencies in other markets.

**Entrepreneurial**

Pioneered the concept of viral PR in the UK. Developed the programme and team to create cost-effective campaigns for clients, including Financial Times, Virgin Mobile, Lastminute.com and Hoover's Online. Developed an anti-jargon campaign for Hoover's that resulted in a sustained 30% rise in site usage and a busy pipeline of subscription sales leads.

| | |
|---|---|
| **Knows media** | Broad understanding of online and offline media channels, including web. wireless, terrestrial and digital TV, radio and print. Has run campaigns designed to maximize client exposure on one or many. For FT.com, helped to create print, web and television advertising campaigns to repos tion the site and drive up levels of traffic from 7 million to 20 million page views per month. |
| **Leads creatively** | Spearheaded the creation of a motivational partner programme to speed consultants' growth within a flat organizational structure. Programme includes an extensive six-part annual review, targeted PR and management training, peer review and partner compensation package including share options. |
| **Career chronology** | **Gnash Communications**<br>Co-managing director from April 2001<br>Board director, October 1999 – April 2001<br><br>**Financial Times**<br>Consultant marcomms manager, FT.com, March 1998 – October 1999<br><br>**Independent Consultant**<br>Clients included Lotus Development Corp (USA); Welsh Slate; and Ketchum PR, April 1996 – March 1998<br><br>**Ogilvy Adams & Rinehart**<br>Account director, pan-European accounts, September 1995 – May 1996<br><br>**Lois Paul & Partners**<br>Senior account manager, Technology March 1992 – June 1995<br><br>**Lotus Development Corp**<br>Consultant, Corporate Communications, October 1989 – January 1992<br><br>**Bronner Schlosberg Humphrey**<br>Account executive, direct marketing, 1984-1987 |
| **Education** | **Emerson College**, Master of Arts, Mass Communication, 1990<br><br>**University of Massachusetts, Boston**, Bachelor of Arts in English Literature and Spanish, Magna Cum Laude, 1984<br><br>**Saint Louis University**, Madrid Spain, Spanish Language and Culture, 1982 |

## BILL FAUST  EFFECTIVE CATALYST

**215 West Hill, Brighton BN1, UK**
**Mobile: 44 (0) xxx xxx xxx, Home: 44 (0) 1273 222222, E-mail: billf@talk21.com**

I bring zest for life to my work and make ideas happen. 14 years of practical, integrated marketing ideas generation for both clients and advertising agencies across the world.

| | |
|---|---|
| **Creative and innovative solutions** | Optimized small budget through pioneering 'viral marketing' campaign for Australia's leading chocolate confectionery Tim Tams. Achieved cult status and notoriety and endorsed by Tim Tams aficionados generating self perpetuating PR.

Created an integrated web presence for Fairfax, one of Australia's leading media groups, that revolutionized the media planner buyer and publishing house relationship. The Internet became the Intranet became the Extranet in a smooth flow of efficiencies. |
| **Entrepreneurial and commercial** | Initiated and implemented the online e-commerce strategy that broadened the potential pet insurance portfolio by £694 million pa an increase of 488%.

Generated innovative one-stop motoring portal strategic interactive offering for News Ltd. Produced a comprehensive business plan encompassing all aspects from costs, head count, potential revenue growth, to the fully specified functionality for the portal. |
| **Project management and relationship building** | Managed direct, indirect reports and 3rd party suppliers at GEIH, CIA & IMP resulting in projects running to time and on budget.

Built long standing client relationships, with Packard Bell and BT through several different roles. |

| | |
|---|---|
| **Strategic thinker** | Wrote the strategy document for Orange's Mobile Portal. Understanding the issues facing the mobile telecommunications market, from the key drivers which influence the use of the mobile platform to new revenue models. |
| | Studied current and future content and services from a customer and commercial point of view to the adoption and advancement of new technology. Produced a strategy document highlighting commercially viable revenue generation in a marketplace that nears full penetration of mobile devices. |
| **Idea generation and implementation** | Co-authored the title *Pitch Yourself* a radical way to sell yourself to potential new employers. Pitched and delivered concept to the publisher, Pearson Education delivered the book in mid-2002. |
| **Career history** | Interim Projects and author of *Pitch Yourself* — 2001 to date UK |
| | **E-Marketing Director GEIH** (part of GE Capital) — 1999–2000 UK |
| | **New Media Director Bates Australia** — 1998–1999 Australia |
| | **Head of Interactive CIA** (largest media independent agency) — 1997–1998 UK |
| | **Head of Sales and Marketing IMP** (top 5 SP agency) — 1996–1997 UK |
| | **Director, Int Marketing YITM** (Yorkshire TV) — 1995–1996 UK |
| | **Account Director U/C/M Ltd** — 1991–1995 UK |
| | **Rights Manager Bayard Presse Paris** — 1990–1991 France |
| | **Advertisement Manager Haymarket Publishing** — 1987–1990 UK |
| **Education** | Business Studies: Bournemouth University. |
| **Languages** | Business French: Acquired for the role at Bayard Presse in Paris |

## MICHAEL FAUST — LEADER WHO BELIEVES 1 + 1 SHOULD NOT ALWAYS EQUAL 2

**Penny Meadow, Cheadle Hulme, Cheshire**
Tel: *44 (0) 161 xxx xxxx*, E-mail: michael_faust@ftnetwork.com

Lateral thinking leader with collaborative yet challenging style. Placing a high value on integrity and trust I question, I persevere and influence others to step change the status quo often going the extra mile.

16 years in international, customer facing roles, integrated marketing and leadership of third party relationships across borders and cultures, gained in both start ups as well as US and Asian blue chip organizations.

| | |
|---|---|
| Creativity, tenacity and reourcefulness | Initiated and delivered a series of symbiotic partnership deals which created Dell's first global sponsorship property with BMW at Le Mans 1999, generating multi million $ global exposure for zero cost and deliveringrobust television campaign over one year in Germany, again, at no cost. |
| | Designed and implemented new collateral strategy that reduced cost y/y 45%, scaled into Asia and USA delivering further regional economies. |
| | By building the world's largest live mobile pager I helped NEC Pagers become ubiquitous in Russia. |
| Commercial acumen & results-driven | At Letsbuyit.com I improved overall e-commerce KPIs through new customer acquisition strategy driving propensity to purchase, decreasing acquisition costs fivefold, increasing repeat purchase nearly 200% and improving overall quality of traffic to site and therefore dramatically driving revenue stream. |
| | Led new business teams to win accounts e.g. Mizuno and Muji, at Hakuhodo. |
| | Delivered results scaled the business and drove key objectives from global sponsorship, maximizing partners to leveraging budgets at Dell. Initiated new working practice for an alliance partnership generating exposure 23x greater than initial Dell investment. |
| Coaching and team building | Excellent at creating climate in which people can learn, by making each individual feel their importance in building consensus. |
| | Being dependable, hard working and energetic I make everyone around me become better and work harder. |
| | *'Excellent leader and manager of agency partners … exceptional in growing others'* – their words not mine. |

| | |
|---|---|
| **Organizational agility and customer focus** | 16 years of customer facing roles all aimed at creating intimacy and delivering ROI both internally and externally.<br><br>Success gained in range of working environments, cultures and style from decentralized Dell matrix to dynamic dotcom 'can do' start-up via blue chip Asian organizations.<br><br>The intangible benefits of the BMW/Dell deal include being one of the highest visited sites on the EMEA intranet demonstrating enhanced staff morale and motivation especially in Germany and France. Merchandise give-aways (several thousand books and cars) delivered enhanced customer affinity.<br><br>Several quotes: *'I do not think you can get a better deal from any other, we shall go ahead...', '...the campaign has been a huge success.' 'GREAT!!!' and '...Dell was really very dominant ...congratulations to a very smart and successful deal...'* |
| **Career history** | **Managing Director, Travelcare    2002–onwards**<br>Full P&L responsibility for UK's largest independent travel agency, £400m+, multi distribution retailer with 370 branches, 1800 staff and 5% UK market share<br><br>**Interim Manager and Author    2001–2002**<br>Strategic European marketing consultancy for establishing internet companes<br>Co-author of *Pitch Yourself*, published by Pearson Education<br><br>**European Marketing Director, Letsbuyit.com    2000–20001**<br>Europe's leading B2C group buying internet retailer. Led 33 strong marketing team and agency partners across 14 markets in creation of internal and external marketing strategy and revenue generation.<br><br>**Head of Corporate Brand Strategy EMEA, Dell    1998–2000**<br>World's leading direct computer company and world's most successful e-business. Led creative, research and media agencies across Europe, budget $40m, helping to define Dell's new e-commerce global positioning<br><br>**Advertising Agencies    1986–1998**<br>From Hakuhodo (Japan's number 2 agency and top 10 global communications agency, 1993–1998), MarketShare (1991 to 1993), YellowHammer (1989 to 1991) to Saatchi & Saatchi (1986 to 1989) |
| **Education** | Bath University, Upper 2nd Class Honours, Economics |

## MARC SCHAVEMAKER COMMERCIAL AIRLINE PILOT (BOEING 737)

Jupiter Laan 64, 1644XS Haarlem, NL
Tel.: 23 (0) 429 xxxx, E-mail: marc@skyport.nl

I continually increase my ability to deal with fast moving complex situations, whilst inspiring confidence in others around me. I have developed a solid foundation in safety procedures and people management.

I worked in industry for six years as a chartered civil engineer prior to becoming an airline pilot 4 years ago.

| | |
|---|---|
| **Ability to lead** | An airline pilot, especially an aspiring captain, must show leadership and commercial awareness in the management of the day-to-day operation, providing a safe, efficient service. The ability to make decisions is based on available information, experience and intuition. I take a leading role and seek to discuss steps I would take in resolving situations that arise. This results in the building of experience and confidence, providing a greater number of appropriate suggestions on operational issues. |
| **Situational awareness and lateral thinking** | It is essential to build a mental model of your surroundings. Continual monitoring of the aircraft systems, maintaining spatial awareness, and constant liaison with all crew including passengers increases my capacity to deal with any event. |
| **Organizational ability and agility** | It is essential to organize my tasks effectively to reduce my workload and increase my capacity. I have the presence of mind and forethought to prioritize and carry out multiple tasks simultaneously whilst maintaining accuracy. This is achieved by planning actions, working logically and thinking ahead. I am then of greater assistance to my captain and can maintain smooth operation of the service. |

| | |
|---|---|
| **Effective communications** | In the aviation industry it is essential to convey and receive information succinctly. I use effective briefing techniques that are imperative for a successful flight from the ground up (and down again). I have an approachable style and carry out my tasks in accordance to the Standard Operating Procedures, whilst liaising with all my fellow crew in an open and co-operative manner, resulting in a reduction of inherent risk and shared knowledge. |
| **Technical and practical aptitude** | I must be fundamentally familiar with the aircraft. I have an awareness and willingness to keep up-to-date with the aircraft systems and handling characteristics. When situations allow, I make the most of handling the aircraft. I study regularly to keep abreast of all relevant material, ensuring I am up to date with all aspects of the aircraft's technical data. This increases my confidence of the aircraft's capabilities, allowing me to be better prepared for all scenarios. |
| **Ability to promote good teamwork** | To maintain a good overall situational awareness and create an effective harmonious team, it is important to create an open and efficient working environment utilizing Crew Resource Management. This maximizes the effectiveness of the whole crew. I must recognize the skills of others and complement them to my own through consultation and delegation, furthering our skill base. The result is to reduce the workload of all crew members, providing an increased capacity to focus on safety and efficiency. |
| **Career history** | **British Airways**    **1998–present** |
| | **NRA & Environment Agency**    **1991–98** |
| **Education** | Civil Engineering degree |

## MARK BAILEY | SEASONED INTERNATIONAL MARKETING PROFESSIONAL

**50 Carabella St, Balgowlah Heights, Sydney, 2062, Australia**
**Tel: 61 (0) 2 99 xxx xxx, E-mail: markb@sydney.com.au**

I thrive on challenges. I am an innovative business builder, re-engineering through people not processes, and taking my clients with me. By bringing together a broad base of eclectic talents and skills to create driven teams, I provide creative and inspiring pragmatic solutions.

For 20 years, I have worked extensively on a national, regional and international basis with a broad range of organizations in both client and agency environments, including successfully developing and some years later merging my own business with a multinational operation.

| | |
|---|---|
| **Innovative solutions** | Created one of the first 'boutique' complete integrated independent marketing communications agencies, Communicate@, incorporating full production and an extensive range of marketing, advertising, planning and execution services. |
| | Developed multi-faceted integrated campaigns to a very diverse range of clients across a broad spectrum of industries, including Reckitt & Colman Group, Digital, Castlemaine Perkins, SmithKline Beecham, Pfizer Healthcare, Roche, Pharmacia & Upjohn, Metway Bank, Parke Davis, CSIRO, Eli Lilly, Woods Bagot, Telstra, Coles Myer, Fosseys and Meditech. |
| | Grew a group of individual specialist businesses in marketing communications, pre-production, production processing and digital cross-platform creation mediums that operated as a total resources unit. Merged Communicate@ with a traditional multinational to create their integrated structure after 8 years of independent operation. |
| **Leading, coaching, developing and exporting skills and learning** | Created and successfully implemented the first business model of its type, assisting with developing skills and personnel to be placed in roles throughout the region in order to further expand these skills and learning into those markets. Leo Integrated became a catalyst for their evolution. |
| | Implemented a greater exchange and dialogue in these evolving specialist business areas internationally, working in sympathy with the developing global vision and a global IPO environment. |
| **Innovative business initiatives** | Helped transform a traditional organization into an industry leader and an enviable growth achiever, when the traditional revenue streams were facing a considerable downturn. |
| | Created a completely new, nationally, regionally and internationally awarded business model for evolving and generating new levels of success and profitability, bringing together and implementing a unique working culture and approach that delivered growth, diversification and a foundation for future success. |
| **Business strategist** | Devised the business strategy. Planned and managed the implementation to create a structure and re-engineer |

the traditional business. Introduced an all-encompassing integrated group of 8 new specialist marketing business units to provide additional services in the areas of sales promotions direct/CRM, digital and interactive, events/PR, healthcare marketing, design, B2B/technology and Communications architecture strategy.

Created a profitable business model dedicated to quality, best-practice delivery, productive resource management, and cross-channel implementation, resulting in a total business revenue contribution that grew from 0 to 40%+ within 4 years.

| | |
|---|---|
| **Integration, resource and team management** | Management of major account groups and co-ordination of creative and other specialist resources to develop and implement strategies for client projects and campaigns. Actively involved in leading new business pitch teams. Part of the Fortune Group, including SSB, DFS & Weston Advertising Agencies, working with these agencies, key mainstream clients, such as Toyota, and with direct clients to provide integrated services. Through a leading below the line/integrated agency specializing in full service provision of complete client needs, including sales promotion, direct/relationship marketing, sports and sponsorship marketing, merchandizing and POS, and sales incentive programmes. Solely responsible for securing Revlon, Ferrero, Chase AMP Bank. |
| **Re-engineering and change management** | Enabled an organization to transform to a stronger customer-centric focus, created a significant cultural and operational change, maintaining core traditional values and enhancing these with revolutionary new values for a significantly evolved environment, working closely with global operations, experience and vision to reinvent best practice. |
| **Career history** | **Leo Burnett/bcom3 – Australia    1997–present**<br>National director integrated solutions<br><br>**Communicate @ Marketing Communications Agency    1989–1997**<br>Managing Partner<br><br>**The Promotional Marketplace    1987–1989**<br>Associate Director<br><br>**Pizza Hut Australasia    1986–1987**<br>Senior Brand Marketing Manager<br><br>**Faberge**<br>Marketing Manager    **1983–1986**<br><br>**Westpac Bank    1981–1983**<br>National Advertising Co-ordinator<br><br>**Nestlé    1979–1981**<br>New Products Officer<br><br>**South British United Insurance Group    1977–1979**<br>Marketing co-ordinator |

## LOUISE MEDLEY  SALES PROFESSIONAL

**The Stables Lock, Yaynings, UK**
**Tel: 44 (0)1592 xxx xxxx, E-mail: lou@freestyle.com**

I care passionately and understand my client's business.

10 years of results-driven sales experience coupled with the ability to deliver commercially viable sales strategies.

| | |
|---|---|
| **Sales negotiation** | The achievement of successful sales whilst maintaining maximum gross profit for the company. I have a sound knowledge of the competition, the parameters they have to work within, and their quoting procedures. I need to ensure the customer purchases from BSS (UK) Ltd without loss of profit margin by using other parameters apart from price to negotiate a successful sale. |
| | This has resulted in healthy gross profit margins and a satisfied loyal customer base. |
| **Ability to spot trends, freestyle frenzie** | I could see an opportunity to develop and build up my own dance company with the view to sell it as a viable and commercial business concern. |
| | To ensure success and the fulfilment of my goal, there were many aspects to be considered: spotting trends, achieving guests figure on the door, the building of an effective and efficient database, ensuring the ambience was measured and matched against the expectations of our guests, the sourcing of new music and venues. I needed to be sure of the best way to approach new guests and existing guests via sales and promotional campaigns, watching carefully the profit and loss ratio. |
| | The company was successfully sold as a going concern in the first quarter of 2001. |
| **Relationship/ partnership building** | I generated and developed long-term relationships based on trust that increased both loyalty and sales of BSS (UK) Ltd. |
| | I did this by maintaining an excellent local knowledge of ongoing and future proposed projects. This has produced a solid customer base that keeps on returning to us time after time, as evidenced by the £2m sales turnover. |

**Customer sales consultancy**

To provide a complete bespoke sales solution for individual customer needs, I must understand their needs and requirements on specific projects and on an ongoing basis to provide the best support and sales service possible.

The production of an individually tailored sales plan in conjunction with client input to successfully combine our products and services to fit neatly to their projects. This in turn has led to an increase in customer confidence and ultimately a greater sales volume exceeding my targets by 20%.

**Internal sales planning and procedures**

To be successful in the field, I need to implement effective and constructive internal procedures that maintain the smooth running of the sales territory.

Careful analysis of sales trends allows me to provide targeted product support optimizing my time in the field.

I pay particular attention to all my quotes ensuring the details are correct.

**Career history**

**BSS (UK) Ltd     1991–2001**
Sales representative

**Freestyle Frenzie     1998–2001**
Set up and sold

## KEN LIVINGSTONE  MAYOR OF LONDON

Running the City of London is my dream job. I am 100% committed to improving the life of each and every Londoner. I lead from the front getting to the root of each issue. I am prepared to stand up to big government for the people of London.

Proven by a 14-year career as a Member of the UK Parliament for the Labour Party and now as the Independent Mayor for London.

**Gaining loyalty and building working relationships**

I give my commitment. I never withdraw it even if I might like to change my mind. I strive to gain a consensus of opinion and act accordingly.

The £7 billion Cross Rail 'Heathrow to Docklands' project demonstrates my total commitment to building successful working relationships across the private and public sectors (central government, city and local councils).

**Long-range thinking**

My experience running the GLC taught me about the need to think many years ahead in turning concepts into structured policies. Transport policies for the Capital are not overnight fixes. To successfully solve the Capital's transport issues I need to exercise interlocking policies that vary in size, manner and approach from 5 to 15 years.

**Employing giants**

I am not afraid to employ giants. The only important issue is to get the very best person to take on the challenge and fulfil the role to its full potential. The London Underground is a classic example. One of my proudest achievements was getting Bob Kiley, a giant in urban transport who reformed the New York subway, to join my team.

**Quick decision making**

I was elected to make a difference. I made a promise to ease the congestion in the Capital and congestion charges for traffic entering the Capital are the answer. I believe in it and believe it is best for London. Government ministers urged me to delay this decision until after the next mayoral election. I went ahead and kept my promise because I believe Londoners have a right to see if it works before they vote again.

| | | |
|---|---|---|
| **Tactician** | Napoleon said 'he sacked generals if they were not lucky'. You need luck and you need tactics. I stood as an independent in the London Mayoral Election. Ten weeks out, four of my five key advisors said I would lose as the press would destroy me. However the press concentrated on my Labour opposition Frank Dobson for the first nine of the ten weeks. Only in the last week did the press turn their attention on me. Luck or Tactics? The right tactics generate luck. | |
| **Dealing with conflict** | Find out the real issue or grievance and solve it. Do not drag it out. Find the common ground. State what is possible. You are left with what is possible and you get straight to the point. | |
| **Career history** | Elected Mayor of London as an Independent | 2000–present |
| | Labour MP for Brent East | 1987–2000 |
| | Elected Leader of the GLC | 1981–1986 |
| | Elected Labour member of the GLC | 1973–1981 |
| | Member of Camden Council | 1978–1982 |
| | Labour Member of Lambeth Council | 1971–1978 |
| | Technician, Chester Beatty Cancer Research Institute | 1963–1971 |
| **Author of** | *If Voting Changed Anything They'd Abolish It* | |
| | *Livingstone's Labour* | |

## DARREN FELL  FOUNDER OF PARTYTASTIC.COM

**Flat 10, The Lofthouse, Docklands, London, UK**
**Tel: 44 (0) 207 xxx xxx, E-mail: darren.fell@partytastic.com**

I am an entrepreneur ever eager and able to grasp ideas with both hands whilst only catching those ideas that generate new and exciting commercial opportunities.

12 years in high-profile technical and international sales roles and more recently founded an innovative Internet-based company, Partytastic, one of London's premier party events company.

| | |
|---|---|
| **Technical aptitude** | Drawing on an inherent technical ability, whilst at COLT Telecommunications, I excelled at clearly understanding business objectives and providing high-level, resilient Internet solutions for customers. This secured sales in excess of £250K. |
| | This is further demonstrated during the start-up phase of Partytastic.com, proving my aptitude to specify and design the Partytastic.com website. A scalable membership-management system to support an exponentially growing membership base. This very system has provided the backbone in marketing, showing clearly the trends of people going to Partytastic parties, and has led to the continued sponsorship of one of the largest drinks manufacturers in the world, Diageo (UDV/Guinness). |
| **Company builder and commercial awareness, Partytastic.com (UK)** | Established a successful events company, Partytastic.com. It has a rapidly growing membership base of 1200, regular events, and an Internet site receiving over 600 unique visitors a day. To achieve the current success, rigorous budgetary control and attention to detail were and are needed. |
| **Integration and consolidation** | The project was to provide an international channel management layer for Colt's operations throughout Europe. I established the international processes and practices to enable successful pan-European Internet hosting deals.. My team exceeded the £5m target by 20%, setting a new standard in the industry for single-point pan-European Internet sales. |

| | |
|---|---|
| **Strategic sales developer** | Created a sales strategy to enable high-value e-commerce activity for our customer base. Built a partnership with a systems integrator. I established best working practices between the facility's company and systems integrator to bid and successfully win business with budgets of a minimum of $500K Australian dollars. |
| **Results-driven** | To employ, train and develop a highly efficient and effective sales team. The primary goal was to generate the entire revenue for the start-up Internet services provider by the direct salesforce and the creation of a reseller channel. This resulted in sales revenues increasing by over 500% month on month for the first year. |
| **Career history** | **Partytastic.com**  2000–present<br>Owner/Managing Director<br><br>**Colt Internet**<br>European Account Manager     2000–2001<br><br>**GX Networks**    1999–2000<br>Account Manager<br><br>**Bates Australia**   1998–1999<br>E-Commerce Director,<br><br>**Morse Computers**    1996–1998<br>Account Manager<br><br>**Cable & Wireless**    1989–1995 |

## JUSTINE COBB OPERATIONS MANAGER

*66 The Look Out, Birling Gap, Sussex, UK*
Tel: 44 (0) 321 xxx xxx, E-mail: justinecobb@justinecobb.co.uk

I get the job done. I don't drop the ball. I cut a clear pathway through demanding commercial projects.

14 years of pragmatic operating management applications in the creative world of fashion and business.

| | |
|---|---|
| **The ability to see clearly through mist** | Set up a clothing-manufacturing unit in Tunisia for the UK-based supplier to Marks & Spencer. Saw through all the bureaucratic red tape resulting in successful launch of the unit on time. |
| | Managed the complete office refurbishment for Infoline Conferences. Managed and co-ordinated the design, building contractors and the architects. This was completed on time and on budget. |
| **Ability to manage successfully** | Remote management of the agents in Tunisia, ensuring delivery dates would be met and approval was achieved from the client Marks and Spencer. |
| | I manage the operational logistics for producing business-to-business conferences from their inception through to completion. |
| **Communicating effectively (written and oral)** | Provide weekly detailed operations reports to the MD of Infoline Conferences ensuring the effective day-to-day running of the business. |

| | |
|---|---|
| **Managing people effectively** | Co-ordinated a team of designers, graders, fabric technicians and production schedulers ensuring we met the high quality standards of Marks & Spencer. Weekly production meetings and one-to-one daily meetings moulded a team that worked effectively and knowledgeably.<br><br>Managed their career progress by encouraging them to develop new skills w th the company with the assurance of my aid at all times and encouraged them to think for themselves and take on the responsibility for their actions. |
| **Career history** | **Infoline Conferences Ltd**    **1999–present**<br>Operations Manager<br><br>**Claremont Garments (M&S supplier)**    **1990–1999**<br>Technical/Quality Manager<br><br>**Jaeger Tailoring Ltd**    **1987–1990**<br>Designer/Pattern Cutter<br><br>**London College of Fashion**    **1983–1987** |

## CHARLIE DOBRES CEO OF 'i-LEVEL'

**i-level, 26–30 Strutton Ground, London SW1P 2HR**
**Tel: 44 (0) 207 3402 700**

I love my family more than I love my work. I have a life and, in getting the balance right, my work is all the better for it. This is the only way I know how to work. I understand marketing, I understand business planning, and I understand people. I seem to be able to get the best out of people. I motivate them. They make the company work. The results follow naturally when you get it right. I don't mind failing, but I do hate it when people haven't tried. My skill is as a company Chief Executive Officer and entrepreneur.

| | |
|---|---|
| **Business builder** | Cofounded i-level plc in late 1998 on a shoestring budget. With my business partner, built the agency up to be the UK No.1 online media agency within one year, where it remains. Made a profit in every year of operation, including the hard times. Zero staff turnover to other agencies in the whole three-year period. |
| **Opportunist** | Despite gaining one of the UK's first BSc degrees in marketing in 1983, I went off to form a band and came quite close to 'making it'. You'll have to ask London Records what went wrong. Eventually came upon advertising as a suitable industry for my skills at the tender age of 26 (I'm 40 now). |
| **People under-stander** | Work/life balance – i-level is run according to these principles. Except in dire emergencies, I don't approve of weekend or late-night working. If this persists, it means that either the company is taking the piss with the workload, or that the employee is not organized well enough – both need fixing. |

**Inspiration**

'Our deepest fear is not that we are inadequate. Our deepest fear is that we are powerful beyond measure. It is our light, not our darkness that most frightens us. We ask ourselves: "Who am I to be brilliant, gorgeous, talented, fabulous?" Actually, who are we not to be? Your playing small doesn't serve the world. There's nothing enlightening about shrinking so that other people won't feel insecure around you. We are all meant to shine, as children do. We were born to make manifest the glory that is within us. It's not just in some of us; it's in everyone. And as we let our own light shine, we unconsciously give other people permission to do the same. As we're liberated from our own fear, our presence automatically liberates others.'

*Nelson Mandela*

**Career history**

CEO founder, i-level plc      1998–present

General Secretary, Internet Advertising Bureau      1997–1998

MD Low Interactive      1995–1997

Account Manager Lowe Howard Spink      1990–1995

## RICHARD DAVIES OWNER AND MANAGING DIRECTOR OF GOOD TECHNOLOGY

332b Ladbroke Grove, London W10 5AH
Tel: 44 (0) 207 565 0022, E-mail: Richard.davies@goodtech.co.uk

**Minding the gap**

I have spent much of my working life proving to others that not only was there a gap in the market but, importantly, also a market in the gap. From my early years as a graduate trainee within the music industry, to the founding and running of my own business, it has been a recurring theme in my life.

Ensuring a commercial opportunity gets realized is often overlooked as a skill, but in my view it's as important (if not more so) as the original idea. If I had a motto (which I hasten to add I wouldn't), it might be something along the lines of, 'Don't sit there talking about it, do it!'

The single most important thing to me is to try to understand, anticipate and motivate people. I may be paranoid, but it helps – ensure everyone that counts is on your side and is working with you and not for you.

I surround myself with those that can do the job better than me.

An obsessive fear of failure constantly drives me.

**Managing creativity**

This enabled me to develop my skills as a team player, co-ordinating those responsible for the creation and delivery of the product to the consumer. This provided me with my first taste of the commercial world and how to deal with that most unpredictable commodity, creative talent!

**Being my own boss**  This has given me the experience in every aspect of running a company, most notably building a team and dealing with the everyday people-management requirements.

It has taught me to question constantly what I am doing and to learn from my mistakes.

Finally, it has instilled self-belief and a determination to succeed.

**How?**  A strict set of values that I adhere to at all times:

- People focused
- Challenging convention
- Informal
- Discipline

**Career history**

| | | |
|---|---|---|
| **MD and owner Good Technology** | 1994–present | |
| **Marketing Manager MCA Records** | 1990–1994 | |
| **Biochemistry degree, UMIST** | 1987–1990 | |

**JACK GRATTON** CEO OF MAJOR PLAYERS LTD

**73–75 Endell St, London WC2H 9AJ**
**Tel: 44 (0) 207 836 4041, E-mail: jack@majorplayers.co.uk**

Caution: rainmaker at work!

My style is built upon classic northern Protestant ethics of hard work, hard play. My pillars and values show fun, professionalism, trust, high morals and sharing.

These statements sum up my career and also my aspirations.

My background is both corporate (Mobil Oil graduate trainee) and latterly entrepreneurial.

My three years in the corporate life didn't suit me, although I raped and pillaged as much knowledge as I possibly could and left with great mentors on how and how not to build brands and get the most from people.

My next three sponge years were spent in a fast-growing marketing services agency, where I acted as a catalyst to one of the brightest, yet fatally flawed, men alive. I learnt how to build a strong team, pull together all their skill sets, and genuinely make the sum of the parts better than the individuals.

That was my apprenticeship; the next 9 years to date have been making rain in the fields of recruitment, training and HR.

I set up, run and own Major Players Ltd, the UK's leading marketing and services recruitment consultancy.

I take my risks outside work on motorcycles, not with people's careers inside!

# How the EP answers a job brief

The following job description and tailored Elevator Pitch was for a regional sales manager.

A full job description was analyzed to ascertain what qualifications and transferable assets the company required.

There is a prerequisite qualification for this position the applicant must be a current registered and qualified veterinary nurse with a minimum of seven years' experience in practice. You will see how this has been covered in her Personal Promise.

A detailed knowledge of selling into the veterinary practices is a further requirement. This too is highlighted in her Personal Promise via the introduction of the most significant Transferable Assets. This will be further elaborated and evidenced in the Elevator Pitch used to answer this job brief.

## JOB DESCRIPTION

**Job title:** Sales Manager

**Location:** Field and Office based

**Reports to:** Sales Director

**Purpose of role:**

➡ Provide a direct influence in practices to endorse the products and brands.

➡ To communicate the benefits of the brand and product range resulting in increased recommendations, sales and distribution throughout practices in the region.

**Responsibilities:**

➡ Develop and maintain high levels of comprehension of the products and their uses coupled to the business initiatives through training and current market activity.

➡ Represent the company to veterinary practices as a partner of choice.

➡ Development of strategic product and sales plans for both the practice and the consumer.

➡ Implementation of the company's sales and marketing activities:

➡ Set practice objectives for the coming year.

➡ Deliver professional sales support to meet set objectives.

➡ Continual monitoring.

➡ Represent the company at the industry conferences and events.

➡ Accurate and current records for all practice in the region.

➡ Work and perform to the key performance indicators.

➡ Work within the agreed budgetary parameters.

**Qualifications:**

➡ Veterinary nurse with a minimum of 7 years' experience.

➡ Excellent knowledge of small-animal and equine veterinary practices.

➡ Previous sales environment, preferably selling directly to veterinary practices.

In essence, the role is a field-based consultative sales position. Laura, who applied for this role needed to use Transferable Assets that portray relationship-building and consultative-selling techniques.

The role requires a measured and intellectual approach. It stresses the importance of partnerships, relationships, strategies, customers and the ability to influence.

After careful analysis of the job description, Laura successfully highlighted the following Transferable Assets on her Elevator Pitch.

⟹ Commercial awareness

⟹ Building and influencing relationships

⟹ Effective and efficient communicator

⟹ Ability to negotiate

⟹ Organizational agility

## LAURA NEILSON  PET INSURANCE SALES REPRESENTATIVE

**Helicopter House, Merryfield, Nr Taunton, Somerset**
**E-mail: Laura@aelsewhere.co.uk**

I have a calm and considered approach to my life. Proven relationship builder and qualified veterinary nurse of 11 years. If I could, I would ride my horse to work.

| | |
|---|---|
| **Building and influencing relationships** | I actively built strategic partnerships where we become the insurance company of choice. I had to ascertain which practices were forward-thinking and insurance-minded.<br><br>This led to support via product and in-house staff training, helping the practice staff become more knowledgeable about how pet insurance can be beneficial to both the pet owners and the practices. The staff became more confident in the recommendation of pet insurance to their clients. 444 out of 700 practices in the region became strategic partners. |
| **Effective and efficient communicator: professional teaching qualification** | Certificate in City and Guilds Coaching & Assessing Individuals. This is awarded to those teaching and working with candidates for their vocational NVQ (National Vocational Qualification). |
| **Commercial awareness** | I set the promotion and advertising budgets by analyzing practice trends and deciding where the marketing budget could be best used.<br><br>The monies were used to produce practice brochures, sponsor open days and produce advertising campaigns. This resulted in an incremental increase in the number of pet insurance policies sold via the participating practices |

| | |
|---|---|
| **Ability to influence** | I had to gain the required shelf space to promote the insurance products in practices throughout my region. Matching the practice needs to the features and benefits and back-up systems of the product ensuring a smooth flow of efficiencies. Provisions were made for both an award/incentive scheme for the staff and the practice, as well as ensuring efficient running of back-end processes, for example on receipt of a claim payments being made to the practice within 48hrs etc. |
| **Efficient marshalling of resources** | To lead and ensure the smooth running of a team of 7 nurses in a busy mixed country practice.

Benchmark similar practices around the country. Looked at previous two years' vet practice management (who does what, where, when, why). Found seasonal trend.

Developed new staff rotas. Created optimal business mix. Freed up additional 20 hours a month of time for every four employees.

An efficient practice where vets could be vets. Ensured nursing staff available for theatre, consulting, laboratory, hospitalized patients, practice administration including small-animal claims forms, nursing rotas, and on-call out-of-hours duties. Made time available for practice nurses and resources for the dispensing of drugs and the teaching of student nurses. |
| **Career history** | **GEFI (part of GE Capital)**   1998–2001<br>Regional Veterinary Manager<br><br>**The Veterinary Group**  1989–1998<br>Head Veterinary Nurse |
| **Professional qualifications** | Veterinary Nursing Diploma<br>Certificate in City & Guilds Coaching & Assessing Individuals |

chapter

# Summary and conclusion

The job market has changed hugely over the last couple of decades and promises to continue doing so. The 21st century is offering more challenges than we ever could have anticipated. There is one simple thing that has not changed over the centuries, our own curiosity and exploration of our surroundings, from physical features to academic understanding and the thirst for knowledge. Our ambition to understand how and why things work and how to get there even more quickly than we had before.

Use of technology in the business environment has leapt forward touching all our lives whatever industry or job function we are pursuing. These technological advances have changed the way our careers will progress in the present and future. The careers we follow have taken on new and different meanings. Mankind has explored avenues in the fields of science and business that once would have been deemed impossible. These advances will, of course, continue.

Demands from the employers have changed. The idea of the career for life is no longer on offer for a majority of the workforce in today's environment. There are of course, a minority of exceptions. Permanent positions are offered but according to industry sources the average time spent in a general marketing position, for example, is just a little over two years.

Employees' demands have also changed. You are not in general looking for a job for life in one company. You are looking for a career and the development of that career. You will move and gain experi-ence in many roles.

This encourages employers to look for different skill sets than in the past. The changing business climate has led them to analyze their activities. They then decide which core competencies and the ratios of these it had and would need to perform at an optimum business level.

With all these changes taking place, the CV has been a constant feature of the employment scene. There have been numerous changes in its layout and the emphasis placed on different aspects of careers. But fundamentally, the structure is the same now as it was 100 years ago at its conception.

The time has come for major re-engineering from the ground up of the CV. Quite simply, it does not answer the needs of today's employers or employees.

Why has this one aspect of our careers stubbornly not changed with the times and not died a death becoming of such an antiquated tool?

It has now, with the birth of the Elevator Pitch. This is the personal sales strategy document designed to meet the requirements of today's working environment and meet all of our needs, wants and desires.

How will this potentially change our lives?

## The candidate

You move from selling yourself to stirring the employer to crave and want to buy your capabilities.

A person using an Elevator Pitch shows they embrace change and turn it to their advantage. You analyze and understand fully what is required for the roles you are applying for.

You become better placed to position yourself in the direction you want to go.

## The recruitment services industry

The Elevator Pitch has the potential to change the way the recruitment services industry looks to service their clients.

The Elevator Pitch encourages the recruitment services industry to look at a candidate's Transferable Assets as opposed to the current industry sector and profession within it. It encourages them to look at someone's whole career as opposed to just a small portion. The result is a better service to both their clients and the candidates creating a more efficient, cost effective employment process for all concerned.

However, changes are taking place. Some recruitment agencies are already embracing the ideas enshrined in the Elevator Pitch. They are trailblazing the way.

As Carl Poplett, consultant of Technology Marketing Recruitment, says:

**"We all need to be a little more open minded and more flexible in our approaches."**

## The employer

The employer gains by receiving more information than ever before in a shorter and more concise document.

The hard work of reading then deciphering personal career information is avoided. Gone are the days when the employer has to break the code of your CV. The Elevator Pitch is clear and defines your edge, showing instantly how you benefit the organization.

At a mere glance, they know who you are and how you do it.

The emphasis is placed on future performance, not the past. Greater awareness can now be placed on Transferable Assets during the entire selection process.

# The final rallying cry

It is always nice to think we may have made our own small contribution to helping you find and secure that great job in a more enjoyable and exacting fashion. We hope you enjoy zagging when the world zigs.

Our own decision to share the Elevator Pitch with you began in the summer of 2001. We had developed a number of prototypes in response to our frustration with the standard CV. I met with Roger Wilcher, a colleague who I first knew at the Lloyd Group Recruitment Ltd. I shared with Roger one of my early Elevator Pitches.

He said, 'Bill I'm surprised no other candidate has sent me an Elevator Pitch. Which book does it come from?'

Several other people, both in the headhunting and HR fields, also asked the same question.

## Now you and they know!